Rafa Benitez began his football coaching career at Real Madrid before going on to manage Real Valladolid, Osasuna, Extremadura and Tenerife. But it was at Valencia where he really made his name, managing the club to the Spanish La Liga title twice – in 2002 and 2004. Appointed manager of Liverpool in 2004, in Rafa's first year in charge he delivered the Champions League trophy, courtesy of an astonishing second-half comeback against AC Milan that came to be known as 'The Miracle of Istanbul.' His first time at Anfield also brought four consecutive seasons in the Premier League top four, the European Super Cup in 2005, and the FA Cup and Community Shield in 2006. But it was the Champions League record which marked him out as an absolutely outstanding operator – he won it once, finished runner-up once, and reached another semi-final and another quarter-final. Benitez left Liverpool to join Inter Milan in 2010, where he won the Italian Super Cup and FIFA Club World Cup, before he departed Italy in 2011. In November 2012 he was appointed Interim Manager of Chelsea for the remainder of the season.

Rafa Benitez was assisted in the writing of this book by **Rory Smith**, a football journalist with *The Times*.

CHAMPIONS LEAGUE DREAMS RAFA BENITEZ

with Rory Smith

headline

First published in Great Britain in 2012 by
HEADLINE PUBLISHING GROUP

First published in paperback in 2013 by
HEADLINE PUBLISHING GROUP

3

Cataloguing in Publication Data is available from the British Library

ISBN 978 0 7553 6364 3

Typeset in Bliss Light by Avon DataSet Ltd, Bidford-on-Avon, Warwickshire

Printed and bound by CPI Group (UK) Ltd, Croydon, CR0 4YY

Headline's policy is to use papers that are natural, renewable and recyclable
products and made from wood grown in sustainable forests. The logging and
manufacturing processes are expected to conform to the environmental
regulations of the country of origin.

HEADLINE PUBLISHING GROUP
An Hachette UK Company
338 Euston Road
London NW1 3BH

www.headline.co.uk
www.hachette.co.uk

Acknowledgements

To all the people who dreamed with us during our Champions League adventures.

With special thanks:

To my father, who would have enjoyed each and every one of these games.

To my wife, Montse, and my daughters, Claudia and Agata, who inspire and motivate me to keep on fighting every day.

To my mother, Charo, and to my brother and sister, Curro and Charo, as well as the rest of our family, both on my side and Montse's: they may live far away, but they are always here with us.

To my staff, those coaches who stood alongside me in those moments and those who are still with me today, for their invaluable help.

To those who have made this book possible, those people who continue to help me every day, Owen, Chris and Juan Francisco, for their patience.

To our friends, Richard and Frankie, Liverpool fans who have accepted me into their homes and their lives as one of them.

To Jonathan Taylor at Headline and David Luxton for their help and support with this project, and to Rory Smith, for his help with writing the book.

I will never forget the personal side of Liverpool Football Club, those people who always added human joy to our success: the people who greeted us every day at Melwood with a smile and kind words of encouragement, or those at the Academy who took such pride in our triumphs.

To David, Rick and the board members at the time who trusted in us and helped us in any way they could.

To the players, all of them, but a special mention for those who were, perhaps, not so famous, but were fundamental in helping us to achieve our objectives.

And of course to the fans, those who live in Liverpool and the millions who supported us from a distance, for all the kindness they have shown me.

All of you are in my heart and in my memory. Because of all of you, and thanks to all of you, we could dream. As Bill Shankly said, we could make the people happy.

Maybe, for many of you who read this book, one of the nights described is the most important of your life; maybe one of them will always be in your memory. Nobody can take that away from you.

Thank you, for everything.

Rafa Benitez

I owe an enormous debt of gratitude to David Luxton and Jonathan Taylor, for taking a chance and asking me to be involved; to Rafa, for making this all much easier than it might have been; to Steve Hothersall, Paul Joyce, Dominic Fifield, Ian Herbert, Dominic King, Sam Wallace and Tony Barrett for their help and guidance; to Tim Hallissey and Tony Evans and all at *The Times* for their patience and perseverance; to Owen, for his encouragement, both gentle and not-that-gentle; to Robert, Rachel and my mum, Alison, for their support; and, in particular, to my dad, Rod, for his implacable pedantry in the face of overwhelming apostrophes. Most of all, though, I would like to thank Kate, for her forbearance, her understanding, and her bottomless reserves of love and coffee.

Rory Smith

Contents

Prologue

EVEN NOW, MANY YEARS ON, THE MESSAGES STILL COME every week. Some are delivered as letters to my home, some arrive as emails, others as comments on my website. There are two or three a day, at least, often many more. Some come with a shirt, a scarf or another memento. Some are handwritten, some in Spanish, some in English, where it is not a first or even a second language.

They describe those nights in Istanbul, in Madrid and Milan, in Barcelona. They discuss Luis Garciá's goal against Chelsea, or Steven Gerrard's strike against Olympiakos. Some touch on the disappointment of Athens, but the joy the journey to Greece brought. They remember penalties scored and penalties saved. They recall songs being sung and flags flown.

Each memory is personal, unique, but almost all of them have one phrase in common, starting the letter or rounding off the email.

Almost all of them, they say, have been written from the heart, to thank me for the best night of their lives.

My response is always the same: it is much safer to say the best night *apart* from your wedding night, in case your wife or your husband is around.

But it is impossible not to be touched, not to be moved by the thought that all that we achieved in our six years at Liverpool brought so much happiness to so many people, all around the world. It is humbling to think that so many were biting their fingernails as we held on to beat Juventus, that so many celebrated that night when Real Madrid were put to the sword at Anfield.

There is another phrase that is common to most of the messages I am sent, and it is one that I hear regularly, too, when supporters stop me in the streets of Liverpool, London or Madrid, wherever I am. They want to thank me, they say, for giving the club – and the fans – their pride back.

It is an appropriate word: pride. In the course of those six years, I think we restored Liverpool to where it belongs, among the greatest clubs in the world; once more, the most famous teams in Europe dreaded the thought of a trip to Anfield, 45,000 people standing in unison, lifting Liverpool up, sweeping us to victory. All of football's elite faced us in the course of my time there, and all of them were beaten.

That we were able to help, that we were able to play a part in placing Liverpool back on their perch, that I was granted the privilege of working for such a special club, is something of which I, too, am enormously proud.

The memories I have of my time at Anfield are ones I will always cherish, as much as any of those supporters who have been kind enough to write to me.

The night when Yossi Benayoun's header gave us victory in the Bernabéu, against the club I supported as a child, played for as a teenager and where I started my career as a coach. Seeing Craig Bellamy tee up John Arne Riise to conquer the Nou Camp, or Fernando Torres swivel his hips and, with one swing of his right foot, give us the lead against Arsenal.

The sight of the massed ranks of our devout supporters, 2,000 of them, chanting my name before we hosted FC Porto, demanding I remain manager. All of those games against Chelsea: Luis Garciá's goal, Daniel Agger scoring at the Anfield Road End, Dirk Kuyt's winning penalty, Fabio Aurelio's free kick in that incredible 4–4 draw, Eidur Gudjohnsen's miss.

Beating Madrid and Manchester United in the space of four days, dispatching one 4–0 and the other 4–1, a week I think will never be repeated.

And then, of course, there is Istanbul.

The majority of the letters I receive touch on what happened on 25 May 2005, on that heartbreaking first half, on what happened at half-time, on the six minutes when everything changed, on the torture of extra time, on the explosion of joy when Jerzy Dudek, his legs wobbling, saved that final penalty, on the celebrations that followed.

One letter, particularly poignant, called it 'a night that made being a lifelong Liverpool fan worthwhile'.

Another fan enclosed an account of his journey to the Ataturk Stadium that night, what he recalled of the game, and his delight afterwards. 'On Wednesday 25 May 2005,' he wrote, 'in the North Stand, in block 307, row 29, seat 366, I dreamed. We all dreamed together. And I don't think I will ever, ever know a dream like this one again. Ever.'

I keep all of those letters, those personal recollections of private experiences. It is impossible to be Liverpool manager for six years without coming to realise quite what the club means to its supporters, not just those in the city, but to all of those who look to Anfield for hope and inspiration around the world.

Fresh from winning La Liga for the second time with Valencia in the summer of 2004, as I prepared to take over at Anfield I did not simply spend my time examining the squad and analysing potential signings: I had an entire language and culture to learn.

Montse, my wife, concentrated on studying the history of the city and of the club, offering me a potted version while I hurriedly tried to improve my English from the Beatles' *Red Album* and *Blue Album*. At that stage, I was not quite aware of how much the Scouse accent would change the words I was hearing.

Montse and I learned about Liverpool as a place. It is a fascinating story, from its roots as a thriving port to the problems of the Second World War and the 1980s, but it is one that is only really possible to appreciate, to understand, once you have experienced it first-hand, when you have met the people and found out about their lives. Needless to say, it was the same with the club. I knew that Liverpool Football Club was special. I did not know quite how special until I arrived.

The fans were warm and welcoming from my very first day. The city of Liverpool soon became my family's home, and it has remained that way. When I left the club, in 2010, and moved to Internazionale in Milan, my daughters were counting down the days until they could return to their home on the Wirral. The smiles on their faces when they came back to England were amazing. Agata, my youngest daughter, was born in Valencia, but if you ask her where she is from, there is no doubt in her mind, none whatsoever. 'Liverpool,' she replies proudly. The idea that she is from Spain does not make sense to her. She is a Scouser now.

That will not change. This city is our home. My family is settled in West Kirby, thanks to the kindness of the people in this part of the world. And the club, too, retains a special place in all our hearts. Even after my time at Anfield came to an end, I have followed the results of the team and made sure I am abreast of all the latest news, and I hope that their future can be as bright as their past. It would be impossible to do anything other than watch out for how they are doing: I cannot pick my daughters up from school without one of the other fathers coming across and discussing the most recent results, updating me on the rumours of possible signings, asking for my assessment of a certain player.

That is what Liverpool is, of course: not a passing interest, but an enduring passion. It means so much to the supporters. I could never have imagined that they would take me, someone born thousands of miles away, to their hearts to such an extent that even long after I left the club, they remember me so fondly.

I am often asked if I can pick a favourite moment of my time at

Liverpool. Istanbul, naturally, but there are many more: that victory at Old Trafford, at the home of our fiercest rivals; or winning at San Siro against Inter Milan, the Italian champions; or eliminating Barcelona, the finest team in the world, the reigning European champions, after beating them on their own territory. There is the FA Cup final in 2006, of course, and seeing Real so emphatically routed at Anfield.

There are so many games. By the end, perhaps, there were almost too many. I remember a little about all of them, snapshots of goals and brief, fleeting moments, and they are intensely happy memories, but the roll-call of victories is so long that, maybe, some of the details might be lost over time.

That is the idea of this book. It is not just a memoir of all that Liverpool achieved in Europe in our six years on Merseyside – all of those famous nights under the floodlights, all of those epic trips to the great cathedrals of the game, in Spain and Italy, in Holland and Germany and Portugal and France – but an attempt to answer some of the questions I am asked about those games.

Many fans want to know how we did it, what the secret was that enabled a team built at far less cost than most of its rivals to punch above its weight for so long, to become a force so feared at home and abroad.

The explanation, of course, is broadly a simple one: sheer hard work, from the coaching staff, the analysis team, the scouts, the players, from everyone at the club.

The inner workings of a football team, though, remain a mystery to many fans. I hope this account will offer a little insight into how we went about not simply winning matches, but reaching the very pinnacle of European football, from the meticulous preparation for every game, making sure we had left nothing to chance as we attempted to stifle our opponents, to find their weaknesses, to exploit their flaws, to control our own destiny, to the intense work undertaken in training and the months of planning to strengthen our side in the transfer market.

Each of those nights, each of those victories, which live so long in the memory, were not days in the making but weeks, often months and even years. I would spend hours at my desk at Melwood, our training ground, or at home, watching videos of our recent perform-ances, to see how we could improve, as well as footage of our opponents, to work out a way to beat each and every one of them.

I hope some of that is captured here too: how each rival was treated differently, how we adapted our tactics to suit the occasion and trouble the opposition, and just what those tactics were. Not just how we achieved all that we did, but why.

Perhaps, only now, with the benefit of time, is it possible to understand the magnitude of those six years. Perhaps it is only in hindsight that it all comes into focus. Those nights are still fresh in the memory, but they seem ever more distant now, so fast does football move, so quickly do things change.

It seems fitting, then, to attempt to look back on the night Liverpool stormed the Nou Camp and conquered the Bernabéu, the silencing of the San Siro and the dashing of Chelsea's dreams of European domination, not once but twice, and all of the other memories the Champions League gave us, all of the moments that neither I nor the fans will ever forget, that still prompt supporters to write letters all these years on.

There are so many games to consider. I have chosen those which are most special to me for particular attention, a guide to our thinking, to the tactics and systems and ideas which made all of our dreams reality. I hope they answer your questions. I hope they put a smile on your face. I hope they bring back happy memories. They certainly do for me.

1

Champions of Europe

JUST WHEN EVERYTHING SEEMED LOST, THE SINGING STARTED.
On three sides of the vast, open bowl of the Ataturk Stadium in
Istanbul our fans rose as one, red and white scarves held high above
their heads, defiantly bellowing our anthem. 'You'll Never Walk
Alone'. Beneath them, eleven players, on the cusp of the forty-five
minutes that would define their careers, their lives, walked onto
the pitch.

A place in history awaited.

We were three goals down to AC Milan in the final of the
Champions League, the biggest game any player, any manager, can
be involved in. And it had all gone horribly wrong, right from the
very first whistle.

We had conceded within a minute, seen our playmaker hobble off
injured, and then watched in horror as our Italian opponents, widely
regarded as the finest side in Europe, ran home two more goals.

It was over. We were beaten before half-time. Liverpool's first European Cup final for twenty years, the culmination of a journey full of courage and joy and hope, would end in bleak despair.

These are the moments that measure you as a manager. The times when the players have lost faith, when their confidence is shattered, their belief washed away in a tide of embarrassment, disappointment and regret. These are the moments when all the work you have done over the course of a season, a career, bears its reward.

Those players who stood at the centre of that vast bowl, watched by 50,000 Liverpool fans, had not been sent back onto that pitch instructed to limit the damage or avoid further humiliation. They had not been allowed to think that all was lost.

Half-time offered us just fifteen minutes to convince them that there was hope, however distant, that there was a chance, however slim. We did all we could to show them that there was a way, that there was no reason to give up, to prove to them that we had a plan. And after all that had happened in that dispiriting first half, they believed.

It would be too much to say that we had planned to score three goals in six minutes.

We knew, though, that if we could score the first goal of the second half, we stood a chance. We would be back in the game. If we scored first, I had told the players, anything could happen. We knew that we could stop Milan, that we could right what went wrong in the first half. And we knew that we could hurt them too. We knew how we could come back from the dead.

We would introduce Dietmar Hamann for Steve Finnan. The German was detailed to hold the midfield together, allowing Steven Gerrard to make the bursts into the penalty area. That brought our first goal, the captain meeting a cross from John Arne Riise with a powerful, emphatic header. Suddenly, our fans stirred. Steven raced back to the centre circle, urging his team-mates and the supporters on.

We told Luis Garciá, Gerrard and Vladimir Smicer, brought on as a first-half substitute for the injured Harry Kewell, to try to exploit the spaces around Andrea Pirlo, Milan's deep-lying playmaker. Four minutes later, that plan also bore fruit. Hamann laid the ball off to the Czech. He hit a low, swerving shot, which Milan Baros, our striker, leapt to avoid. The strike squeezed between Dida, Milan's goalkeeper, and his right-hand post, and ignited the evening.

Milan were teetering, crumbling. At half-time they had been certain of victory. They'd had one hand already placed on the European Cup, the most coveted prize in club football. And now they found themselves trying to hold back a red tide.

Gerrard, totally liberated from his defensive duties now, powered into the box again. Milan's defence melted away. Baros laid the ball into his path. Gerrard drew his leg back. This would be three. This was our equaliser. On the bench, we held our breath. And then he tumbled to the floor, tripped by Gennaro Gattuso, Milan's defensive midfielder.

Penalty.

Xabi Alonso would take it. It would be his responsibility, his opportunity to complete the most remarkable comeback of all time.

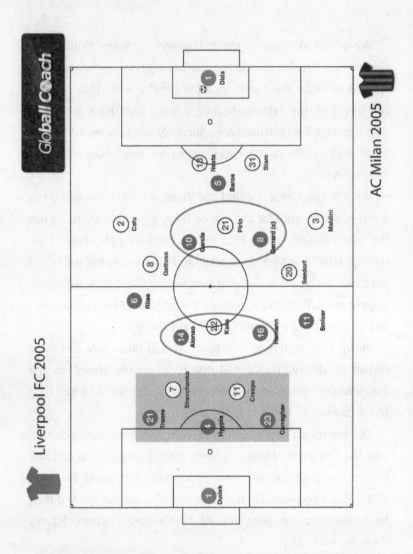

By switching to a back three and placing Hamann alongside Alonso in central midfield, we would be able to control Shevchenko and Crespo, as well as cutting off the runs of Kaka. In attack, Luis Garcia and Gerrard were told to play either side of Andrea Pirlo, looking for second balls and not allowing the midfielder time to pick his passes.

All the rest of us could do – the coaches, the technical staff – was look on, entirely powerless.

He missed. Dida sprawled low to his left to claw the ball away. Alonso pounced on the rebound. He crashed his shot into the roof of the net, wheeling away to be buried under a pile of jubilant, ecstatic team-mates.

On the bench, we could barely believe our eyes. My staff and our substitutes streamed around me, celebrating, dancing, jumping. Did we want that to happen? Without question. Did we plan it exactly like that? Not quite.

It had taken six minutes. Watched by the unbelieving eyes of the world, the unthinkable had happened. We had fought back from the dead.

In six minutes, everything had changed.

The players believed. They believed we had a plan. They believed we could beat Milan. They believed we could win the Champions League. In that second half, after those breathless six minutes had drawn us level, we had much more control of the game. Milan began to tire. Ancelotti's team could no longer find the outlets that they had been using to such devastating effect in the first forty-five minutes. They could not supply Andriy Shevchenko and Hernán Crespo. Hamann, as he had been asked, kept Kaka quiet, preventing the runs which had caused us so many problems in the first half.

We might have won it then, with Milan dazed by what had happened, with adrenaline coursing through our veins. Riise went close to scoring a fourth, to rubbing salt in the wound. As the clock ticked, though, the huge effort we had been forced to produce to bring ourselves back into the game took its toll. Milan was not the only team suffering.

We were limited in how we could play. While Milan had four or five players who could make the difference in just a split second, we had just one or two. We had just one substitution left, and our options were not exactly plentiful. One glance at our bench proved one thing: Liverpool did not possess the sort of squad you expect to see in a Champions League final.

Without match-changing replacements or abundant quality, we had to make best use of what we had. We had to keep on working hard to limit our opponents and try to catch them on the counter-attack. We knew we would have to stay compact and narrow when we did not have possession, and try to look for Baros – and, for the final five minutes, his replacement, Djibril Cissé – behind their defence. We had to win set pieces and then look to play the ball forward. There was no point playing the ball short, attempting to pass around Milan. We simply did not have the ability.

There would be no winner in normal time. Both teams, I think, were glad of the break afforded by the whistle that signalled the end of the ninety minutes. We would go into extra time. In that stifling heat, it was far from ideal. Given how our evening had started, it was a miracle we had made it this far.

We still had one or two alterations to make. Milan had brought on Serginho, a speedy Brazilian left-winger, in the final few minutes of normal time, and we had no choice but to move Gerrard to right wing-back to counter him. He did extraordinarily well. They had five in the middle, trying to control things, but we held our ground well.

It worked. We restricted Milan to just one or two chances. Had things worked out differently, Djimi Traore might not have been on the pitch beyond half-time. As it was, he was there, stationed on the far post, to clear off the line when Jerzy Dudek spilled a cross.

We had started to wilt. The comeback had taken so much out of us. We were not playing for penalties, but our first priority had to be not to concede.

I could not have asked more of my players. Jamie Carragher went down with cramp, but played on, through the searing pain.

Milan would have one more chance. There would be one more glimpse of light through our creaking defence that almost rendered all of our energy and effort futile.

Serginho broke free and swung a cross in towards Shevchenko. The finest striker in Europe, perhaps five or six yards out. A glancing header, straight at our goalkeeper. A hand came out, instinctively, to bat it away. The ball fell for Shevchenko, alert, predatory. Three yards out this time. Unmarked. Dudek sprang to his feet. Somehow, he swatted the striker's second effort over. It happened in the blink of an eye.

There were three minutes to go. That was the save that won the Champions League. It is only afterwards that you realise quite how close you have come. Quite how fine the margins are.

The final whistle blew. Penalties. It would all come down to this. A whole season's work, hundreds and thousands of hours on the training pitch, in the analysis suite, scouting opponents, improving our play, everything. Five penalties, for the European Cup.

I walked onto the pitch to begin the selection process of our penalty-takers. My squad was dripping with sweat, their legs aching, their bodies exhausted.

I looked into the players' eyes. They believed.

I had eight names in front of me. Hamann would go first. Then Cissé, because of the power of his shot. Riise had absolute confidence that he should take one. Smicer's quality was his precision. And then Gerrard would be last. Exactly the sort of person you would want when the pressure is so intense. When everything comes down to one kick. One moment.

If we needed them, Xabi Alonso, Luis Garciá and Carra were ready too. Though Xabi was our usual penalty-taker, given the events of the game, I did not want to put him under too much pressure. Garciá's touch was not always the surest. Carra, after a heroic performance, was still suffering from cramp. They would be our reserves, called upon only if the shootout went to sudden death.

I had looked at all eight of them in turn, to see if they had conviction in their eyes. You can see from the way they look, from the way their faces are set, whether they believe they can score or not. If you are convinced, you say you will consider it. If you aren't, you say, 'OK.' You do not want to hurt their feelings. And then you move on to the next.

It was no surprise that all eight of them had confidence. Perhaps they felt the hand of destiny on their shoulders. Perhaps they thought, after all they had been through, that it would be a cruel fate that denied them victory. An hour and a half before, we had lost the European Cup. Now we were still standing, within five penalty kicks of winning it. Of course they had confidence. Of course they believed.

It is easy to say that penalties are a lottery, are all down to luck, but that is deeply unfair. All managers, goalkeepers and goalkeeping coaches prepare for penalty shootouts. An enormous amount of work goes into those ten kicks, for and against.

We knew where we thought Milan's players would aim. We had examined the last half dozen penalties taken by each player and divided the goal into six areas. Each area was given a number. From the goalkeeper's point of view, one is the top right corner, two down the middle and high, three top left. Four is bottom left, five low and central, six along the ground to the right.

Each penalty was annotated with the corresponding number. We had a list for each player – no easy feat, given that in a penalty shootout players who only very occasionally take spot-kicks would be called into action. This is information I have been compiling since I was twenty-six, for almost thirty years, and it is something my coaches – first José Manuel 'Ocho' Ochotorena, then Xavi Valero – are assiduous in doing. It is years of research by a dedicated team. As they say, sometimes you can make your own luck.

So, for example, Shevchenko's list read: four, four, four, four, six. We could not predict where he would go this time, of course, but we knew that he was inclined to go low to the goalkeeper's right.

Once we had submitted our list of penalty-takers, that became my primary concern: making sure Dudek knew the numbers. We had shown him on the laptop prior to the game, had explained where every likely taker could be expected to aim, but under such circumstances it is understandable that sometimes they forget. As each Milan player walked forward, Ocho was frantically signalling to him where to go.

The only part of that penalty shootout which we had not worked through previously were Dudek's theatrics on the goal-line. That was an idea Carra whispered to him as they waited for the shootout to start.

It worked.

Serginho went first for Milan, in front of the massed ranks of our supporters, countless hands locked together in silent, desperate prayer. The Brazilian would normally aim low to the goalkeeper's right. With Dudek bouncing up and down, waving his arms, he sent his shot high above the bar.

As coaches, all you can do now is stand and watch. It is up to the players. Didi Hamann, who had been so disappointed not to start the game, would take our first. His run-up was casual, assured. He stroked the ball into the left-hand corner.

Pirlo, so key to the way Milan play, the man we had worked so hard to shut down. Low, to Dudek's right, as we expected. Saved in zone six.

We were nearly there.

Next, Cissé. I had wanted him for his powerful shot. He elected to side-foot it. Dida went the wrong way. 2–0.

Jon-Dahl Tomasson, a substitute, was next for Milan. He scored, Dudek diving the wrong way, to the Dane's preferred side. He did not conform to our expectations. The system, of course, is not flawless.

Riise, who had been so desperate to take one, so certain of his abilities. Saved. 2–1.

Kaka. More theatrics from Dudek, but to no avail. He went the wrong way. 2–2. The two teams were level. All around us, nerves were shredding.

Vladimir Smicer had to keep a cool head. This would be his last kick of a ball for Liverpool. Calmly, he slotted the ball to Dida's left. 3–2. From that brief moment of fear, now we stood on the brink of sheer, impossible joy.

And then Shevchenko, Milan's fifth and final nominated taker.

On the bench, Ocho was bellowing 'Six, six' at Dudek, all the way down the other end of the field.

Whether he heard or he remembered, he obeyed. Dudek dived low, to his right. Shevchenko attempted a chip, straight down the middle. Out came a hand, to palm the ball away. For a second, everything stopped. Then the players, gathered in the centre circle to offer each other support, raced to the end where Dudek was on his knees, punching the air in delight. On the bench, we embraced.

We had won the European Cup.

'Now you can make me the best midfielder in the world,' Steven Gerrard told my assistant, Pako Ayesterán, as we paraded that giant silver trophy around all four sides of the Ataturk, offering each of our delirious fans the opportunity to share in the unlikeliest of victories.

It had still not really sunk in. The celebrations on the pitch were surreal, almost: absolute ecstasy mixed with utter disbelief.

Straight after the final whistle, we had been forced to worry about medals: incredibly, UEFA only supply twenty-five medals for the winning team, one for each member of the Champions League squad. That meant that all of the coaching staff, the analysis team, the scouts, the physios and the dozens of people who had contributed to that victory would not have any memento for their role in the triumph.

Graciously, Mauricio Pellegrino – a non-playing member of the squad – agreed to give up his medal, having already won the competition with Barcelona early in his career. He then had the presence of mind to gather up the losing medals, awarded to and cast away by Milan's shell-shocked players, in order to present them to all of those people who would not be recognised by UEFA. It was quick thinking by a warm, intelligent man.

I was as delighted as anyone, though perhaps I was not as elaborate in my celebrations as some of the players. It is a mixture of relief – at having won when all seemed lost – and incredible pride at having achieved something you have worked so hard for, over the course of a season, over the course of a career. When you work so hard and you succeed, it feels even better.

I made sure to seek out each of my coaches, all of my staff, to shake their hands, to thank them for their work. There were a lot of hugs. When we met the players, who had raced off to celebrate with the fans, there were more. It was an intensely emotional night, joyous, delighted.

I cannot be certain how long we spent out on the pitch after the trophy had been presented, listening to the fans singing the anthem, celebrating, embracing. By the time we reached the dressing room, the smoke from the fireworks had long since cleared and the ticker tape had been trodden into the pitch.

As manager, the evening was far from over.

The players continued to celebrate in the changing room, with Rick Parry, the chief executive, and the chairman, David Moores. He had tears in his eyes. This was a moment he had dreamed of seeing for so long. Gerard Houllier, the man I replaced, who was at the match as a UEFA observer, arrived to offer his congratulations. The room was full of friends and family, everyone seeking to congratulate the players who had returned Liverpool to their place as kings of Europe.

Steven, the Man of the Match, and I had to go and give ten, maybe twelve, interviews each, as well as a full press conference. There were hundreds of journalists with cameras and laptops crammed into that room. The questions about the future came thick and fast: Steven's, Liverpool's. UEFA had still not confirmed whether we would be allowed to defend the trophy. Would we protest? What did I say at half-time? What was the secret to the comeback?

It was very early in the morning by the time we left the ground – 1 a.m., 2 a.m., I cannot be sure – but the evening was still far from over.

The real celebrations would start at the hotel. We had a private room set aside, where the players and the staff would be joined by their families. There was security on the door and in the middle stood the European Cup, our gleaming prize.

The room was packed, everyone desperate to congratulate us, though more important was the chance to have their photos taken with the real star of the show: the trophy.

I remember bumping into Carra's dad, Philip, and standing there talking to him for a minute. Like his son, Philip has a very strong Scouse accent at the best of times. By this stage, though, at one or two in the morning, he was – to use the English term – quite merry, and to be honest, I had no idea what he was saying. I stood and nodded for a minute, smiling politely at him, desperately trying to work out what he was talking about, before someone pulled me away for another picture.

Only close friends and family were welcome in that room – by invitation only – and at one point I was summoned to the hotel lobby by Richard Green, one of the club's legal counsels. He had come to the game as a corporate guest and he had been invited to come to the hotel to join in the party.

'Rafa, I've got to have my picture taken with the cup,' he told me.

'Come on, come on,' I answered, guiding him towards the door of our private room.

Suddenly, though, an arm appeared. The security man, who did not speak any English, would not let us in.

'I was in there just a moment ago,' I said.

He wouldn't budge. He just shook his head.

Richard was getting agitated. Probably more because he wanted to see the European Cup than because he was worried about me being shut out of the party. 'Do you know who this is?' he asked. 'This is the man who's just won the Champions League!'

'Richard, Richard,' I said. 'It's OK, don't shout.'

'No,' he said. 'We've got to get back in. This is Rafa Benítez!'

The stalemate lasted a few minutes, before the guard eventually relented. We would be allowed back into the party. I could rejoin Montse and her aunt, Carmen, and Richard could have his photo taken. He was delighted to see me allowed back in. He was rather more delighted to get that picture.

It was 4 a.m. by the time I made it to bed. Some of the players chose to go on elsewhere – Milan Baros, Igor Biscan and Vladimir Smicer went to join the fans in Taksim Square, in the centre of the city – and some stayed in the hotel. Steven Gerrard decided only he would be able to keep the cup safe, and so it spent the night with him. It belonged, though, to all of us.

As far as you could see, people were lining the streets. They had clambered up lamp-posts, scaled buildings, sat on top of traffic lights and roofs. They waved from the windows of offices and houses, from the very top of Lime Street Station. They were decked out in red, flying flags, flourishing home-made banners. There was one that stands out for me, that caught my eye as we crawled along, waving from the top of our red double-decker bus.

It read: 'Rafa – the best import since the spud.' That one really made me smile.

Every time we went round a corner, you thought it would come to an end, but the crowds just went on and on. They stood four, five, ten deep, all the way from Queens Drive to Anfield, down Scotland Road and into the heart of the city, rounding the corner to be confronted with the baroque façade of St George's Hall and the Empire theatre, lit from below by spotlights, the backdrop to a sea of people. A hundred thousand camera flashes went off like fireworks in the dying evening light.

They told me afterwards that 750,000 people had been on the streets to watch our victory parade the day after the final. They had come from all over the country to be there, some from different parts of the world. Most unbelievably, they said that some of them were Everton supporters.

I had known celebrations with Valencia, but nothing like this. We were all tired, having not had much sleep, but you have to keep smiling and waving, all the way to St George's Hall, because those people have come out to see you and it means so much to them. It is important not to disappoint anyone.

We had flown back from Istanbul that morning, on a flight packed with players, staff and relatives, as well as the press corps and some of our corporate guests.

I had given a brief press conference in our hotel, sitting on a raised dais in a small meeting room downstairs from the main lobby. Outside, it was chaos. Players were mingling with journalists and fans. There were hundreds of people there. The questions kept coming: how many of these players would still be here next season? Should we be allowed back in the competition?

There were more immediate worries: we had to decide which of the players' wives and girlfriends would be allowed on the bus back to the airport with us, and then who would get on the plane. There were so many people who wanted to come with the team: all of the coaches, of course, the rest of the club staff and everyone's families. I had managed maybe four hours' sleep. By 9.30 a.m. I was talking to the press; by 10.30 we were leaving.

The plane back to John Lennon Airport was equally chaotic. Normally, the coaches sit at the front, then the players, then the VIP guests, then the press. That day, we all sat together.

The mood was more relaxed now. Some players slept, others stood around and chatted to their friends. About an hour into the four-hour flight, Steven took the trophy from its seat between Igor Biscan and Jerzy Dudek and passed it down the plane, giving everyone the chance to have their picture taken with it.

I was starting to think about what was to come. We had already drawn up the training schedules for the following season. I have always been the sort who as soon as something has been achieved, begins to look for the next target. That morning, I was thinking about what had to be done if we were to improve on our performance in the Premier League in my second season at Liverpool.

I knew that some of the players who had performed so heroically just twelve hours or so previously might have to be phased out, or even replaced. I knew some of them were starting to come to the end of their Liverpool careers. We needed more power, more pace and more quality if we were to build on the previous night's triumph. And we needed to redevelop our youth system, too, to get the academy to start to produce players once more. We needed to move forward as a team, as a club.

We had ended one long wait. It had been twenty-one years since Liverpool had won their fourth European Cup. In the most unlikely circumstances, we had added a fifth. Now we needed to turn our attentions to restoring ourselves as the dominant force in England. This was a club that needed to be back on its perch.

All of those thoughts left my mind as soon as we touched down. I waited for Steven by the doors, my winners' medal round my neck. He joined me, and together we held the European Cup aloft at the top of the stairs. All of the staff at the airport had come out to meet us, and they responded with a loud cheer. We had all celebrated long into the night – some longer than others – but there was more to come.

We were whisked straight from the tarmac to Melwood, by coach, to drop off our things, and from there we drove to a police station, where we left our cars and boarded our bus for the open-top parade. At the top of Queens Drive, we met a second bus, full of media representatives, and began the slow journey into the city centre.

The bus, as you might expect, was packed. Each of the players had their families there, and I was no different. Montse was on board, and the children too, each of them sharing in that once-in-a-lifetime moment. That was around 7 p.m.

There were more people around Anfield – lining the streets, sitting on top of walls, in trees, hanging from railings – than on an ordinary match day. We soon lost the second bus, swallowed by the crowds. Supporters, banners, flags, as far as you could see.

That was nothing, though, compared to the scene at St George's Hall. It was turning that corner that took my breath away. I was standing behind the players, letting them enjoy the moment they had worked so hard to earn, the moment so few of their peers will ever get to experience, but for a minute I was speechless. I was told later there were around 300,000 people there alone, waiting for hours for our bus to arrive, delirious and disbelieving about the events of the night before.

It was late in the evening when we drove back to Melwood to collect our possessions. The bus driver obviously wanted to get on with the celebrations: he was driving much faster now, no doubt desperate to drop us off so that he could go and join in.

But the roads to Melwood are narrow and a lot of them have low-hanging trees along the sides. The players were still on the top of the bus, and I was worried at the thought of one of them being hit by a branch. I kept telling them to be careful, to watch their heads as we passed another tree. Thankfully, they all survived the journey back in one piece, clambering off the bus with seats as souvenirs of the best twenty-four hours of their lives.

We had made it. The champions of Europe were home.

2

Season 2005–06
Lessons Learned

BY 9 A.M. THE NEXT DAY, LESS THAN THIRTY-SIX HOURS AFTER we had won the European Cup, I was back in my office at Melwood. There was work to be done. There was a season to prepare for.

Melwood is usually bustling with activity, full of the sounds of players chatting and exchanging jokes, staff swapping notes and preparing for training, visitors – sponsors, agents, friends and journalists – coming and going: the usual noise of a place of business.

That Friday, the morning after the night before, it was far more tranquil. The city was only just waking up, still scratching its head, unable to believe what had happened. On the pitches, in the dressing room and in the offices, it was quiet. Peaceful.

Only a handful of us were there, poring over plans for the coming year, our strategy in the transfer market, how we would improve the side. Pako Ayesterán, Paco Herrera, the goalkeeping coach José Manuel Ochotorena and Frank McParland were the only other footballing staff in the building.

I remember bumping into Owen, our chief English scout, on the stairs to my office. It was the first time I had seen him since Istanbul. He was beaming with happiness. He raced up to me and gave me an enormous bear hug. 'We did it, boss,' he exclaimed. 'We did it!'

'Yes, yes, Owen,' I answered. 'Come on. That's enough. We have things to do.' I would have a holiday that year, a week away with Montse and the children at half-term, but that was all. I would not consider allowing myself to rest on my laurels.

The first order of business was to arrange a new contract for Dietmar Hamann. We had initially spoken in January of that year, and had verbally agreed to extend his stay by a season, with an automatic extension of twelve months if he played in twenty-five games, but our form in the league had dipped soon afterwards and it had struck me that he would not be able to play nearly that regularly the following year if we were to progress. I had to call him into my office and tell him that he would not receive a formal contract offer. He was such a loyal servant to the club, and he was devastated.

Hamann, though, had more than proved he had a role to play in the intervening weeks. He came into my office, a little the worse for wear, first thing on that Friday morning and told me, barely before I could speak, that he wanted to stay. It was obvious how much Liverpool meant to him.

'We can make you the same offer,' I told him. 'A year's extension, and an extra year if you play in twenty-five games.'

I was sure he would play in that many fixtures without a problem: with all of our commitments in Europe and at home, we expected to play maybe sixty games every year. I did not want to set the clause too high; I wanted him to be able to make it.

Hamann, though, was unhappy that I had chosen not to play him in Istanbul, just two days previously. He made it clear that he felt he had proved his worth to the club, coming on in the second half to such impressive effect, despite the fact that – at the time – he thought he had not only been named as a sub-stitute in the biggest game of his career, but his last appearance for Liverpool.

'The team comes first,' I reminded him. 'You cannot think about anything else. Only the team. You have to put the team first.'

He wanted to lower the clause that would guarantee a second year, and eventually we reached a compromise. 'We will say that the clause comes into effect after twenty-two games then,' I said. 'That's the best I can do. We will play so many games that it will not be a problem at all.'

We had a deal.

Hamann, of course, was one of the lucky ones. He would be able to stay for another year, perhaps two. There would be others who would not be so fortunate, who would have to endure that awkward conversation, full of doubt and hurt.

In an ideal world, you would only sell the players you have deemed surplus to requirements, the ones that are no longer needed.

Football is more complicated than that, though, especially when you need to raise funds to strengthen your squad. Unwanted players, of course, do not fetch much money, as potential suitors often know you are keen to offload them, strengthening their bargaining position and weakening yours. Every year, one or two of those you would like to keep have to go too.

It is one of the hardest things a manager has to do, to tell players they are no longer needed, that they are in the market. That summer would be full of such difficult, strained moments. Several players who had helped us reach Istanbul, who had each etched their names in history, would have to be told their services were no longer required.

We would say goodbye to Vladimir Smicer, of course, on a free transfer to Bordeaux after his contract expired. Milan Baros, who had worked so hard for us that year, joined Aston Villa. Antonio Nuñez, who had fallen in love with the club and the city and was desperate to stay, was sold to Celta Vigo, in Spain. Telling him that he was no longer required, over the phone, was particularly hard: leaving a team where they will not play is often the best thing for a footballer, but at the time they rarely see things so objectively. The manager, conversely, can only be objective. That is the job you are paid to do.

You have to confront those emotions. I do not enjoy those conversations at all, saying goodbye to talented, hard-working players, but I find the best approach is to be straightforward and honest. It is best for you, and it is best for the player too. In football, there is only one truth: the team has to come first.

* * *

It was already clear what was needed if we were to improve our performance in the league. That was our priority now. We needed to be physically stronger, more imposing. We already knew the sort of players we were looking for, and we had spent the previous six months identifying targets, assessing whether they were realistic and examining our options.

Even with all of that painstaking research, the transfer window is frenzied, frantic. Take Mohamed Sissoko, a player I knew well from our time together at Valencia. Momo's power and pace would help us win more second balls in midfield, and he had a great mentality. The only problem was that Everton wanted to sign him too. They even had a bid accepted. As they were flying out to meet him in Spain, I was on the phone, reassuring him. 'I will have to sign something,' he said, worrying. 'Don't sign a thing,' I told him. 'You will sign for us.' He did, of course. We had the player we wanted. Everton flew back empty-handed.

As well as Momo, we signed Boudewijn Zenden on a free transfer from Middlesbrough, Peter Crouch from Southampton, and Mark González, a pacey winger from Chile, though the rules governing work permits meant he would not be able to join us for another year.

Our first signing, though, would prove to be the most success-ful. We had decided during our first season that we needed a goalkeeper who dominated the penalty area rather more than Jerzy Dudek did, and one who was more confident under the high ball. Pepe Reina, of Villarreal, was just the man, and we moved quickly to secure his arrival.

Perhaps there was a degree of surprise that we had effectively demoted one of the heroes of Istanbul so soon after his crucial penalty save, and those Bruce Grobbelaar-inspired legs which had brought the European Cup back to Anfield, but you cannot let one game change your thinking or cloud your judgment. You do what has to be done.

It was on that day, though, the day Pepe signed for us and we could unveil our summer signings, when our plans seemed to be coming together, that Liverpool's world turned upside down.

That was the day that Steven Gerrard and his agent, Struan Marshall, informed David Moores and Rick Parry that talks over a new contract were over and would not be starting up again. It was the day that Steven released a statement confirming that he wanted to leave his boyhood club, the team he had just led to the European Cup, the side he had felt would help him become the best midfielder in the world just a month or so before.

Chelsea had already lodged a bid, for £32 million. Steven said he was sad and angry that Liverpool, in his view, had not moved quickly enough to draw up a new contract after Istanbul. He had turned down one offer of improved terms and, he told the club, was not prepared to wait for another one.

We met him that night, me, David and Rick. We tried, all three of us, to persuade him to think about what this meant. David offered him the biggest contract in the club's history to stay. Both he and Rick did everything possible to explain to him how much they wanted to keep him, to show exactly how much he meant to Liverpool, and perhaps to make him consider how much Liverpool meant to him. Both were visibly upset by the strain of the meeting. They could not have been more impassioned, more honest.

Steven was not taking this decision lightly. This was possibly the hardest decision of his life and it was easy to see the toll it had taken on him. I told him to go and speak to his family, to see what they wanted, to consider what leaving Liverpool meant. He said he would go away and sleep on his decision.

Such times are a whirlwind. We rushed to release statements, to tell the fans what was happening. Rick confirmed that Chelsea's bid, a British record, had been turned down. I told our website that we did not need to sell Stevie to raise money, that we had players desperate to come and play for the European champions. We did. And we wanted more than anything that they should play with the man who had lifted the European Cup. I wanted all of the fans to know that, and I wanted Steven to know it too.

I do not know what happened with Stevie that evening. I don't know who he talked to, or what was said, or what made him change his mind. All that matters is that he *did* change his mind, that the next morning he withdrew his transfer request. He agreed to sign the contract. He even offered to give up the captaincy, a gesture that was immediately rejected. We had wanted to keep our captain all along. We were not about to throw him away.

A little over a week later, any doubts over where Steven's future lay were completely ended. He scored a hat-trick as we beat Total Network Solutions, the Welsh champions, on a warm summer evening at Anfield, in the game that marked our return to Champions

League action, barely a month since we had won the tournament. All thoughts of leaving had disappeared. Steven and Liverpool would not be the same without each other.

It would have been easy to take our opponents lightly that day. After all, we were European champions, fresh from victory over AC Milan. TNS were not even fully professional.

We were only involved in the first round of the competition because of the confusion in UEFA's constitution over what happened when the team that won the Champions League did not qualify for the tournament through its domestic league. It sounds the most obvious thing in the world, that you should have the right to defend your title, but the rules did not allow us to do so. Only after intense wrangling did common sense prevail, at a price: we would have to navigate three qualifying ties, starting in the second week of July. They would not make it easy for us to win the competition again.

Thanks to Steven, though, we saw off TNS with relative ease. We prepared for the two-legged tie as we would any other, studying videos of their recent games, fine-tuning our tactics to suit the occasion. We could see they were a good side – top of their table – and, when we met some of their staff, we were impressed, but it was hard to assess the level they were playing at.

Such situations can be dangerous. The game had to become part of our pre-season. We had to fit it in around our usual training sessions, slightly altered so that we did not tire the players out. Normally, the day before a pre-season game we will do weights sessions, because we know that after forty-five minutes you can substitute the entire team. In a competitive game, you do not possess such a luxury. We knew it was a much bigger risk.

At such times, the mentality of your players is crucial. Sometimes it is better to find a player with ambition and focus than it is to sign a superstar who does not have the right mindset, who decides he is not interested in anything but the most glamorous games. Everyone wants to play in Champions League games, to be involved in famous nights in front of thousands of fans and millions of people watching on television. Against a lesser-known side, two weeks into July, some would not give their best. There is a balance to be found.

Fortunately, we dealt with both those games professionally. Steven added another two to his hat-trick in the first leg when we made the short journey to the Racecourse Ground, Wrexham – quite a contrast to our previous game away from home, in the Ataturk – and Djibril Cissé scored another. We progressed 6–0 on aggregate, and dispatched FBK Kaunas, of Lithuania, just as professionally, going through 5–1 over the two legs.

CSKA Sofia were our final opponents. A 3–1 win in Bulgaria meant that a defeat by a single goal at Anfield was immaterial. Liverpool, champions of Europe, were back in the competition proper. It had been a long journey, covering thousands of miles. It had taken almost two months, but we were once more where we belonged.

There was still one more player to sign. With Crouch already at Anfield, I knew we would need a winger capable of reliable delivery to get the best out of him. The man we identified was Simao Sabrosa, the Portuguese international, then with Benfica.

Initial conversations, as transfer deadline day approached, were not good. The player was interested, but the club told us they simply could not sell him. The fans, they said, would not accept it. 'Even for twenty million pounds,' one of their directors told the club, 'we just cannot do it.'

When I discussed Simao with Rick, I was surprised when he told me that we could make an offer for him, despite the players we had already signed that season. The deadline was drawing near. We put our bid to the same director. 'Maybe for £18 million,' he said.

It was quite a change from not being able to sell the player at all, for fear of a backlash from their supporters. It was a start, but they would not reduce the price, and we could not match it. The player was sitting on alert, at Lisbon Airport, ready to fly to England to complete the paperwork, but Benfica would not budge. Only a premium fee would cushion the blow to their fans, they said. We could not go higher.

The deal fell apart. It would not be the last time we would meet Benfica, or Simao, that season. He would return to haunt us.

It was a desperately disappointing season in Europe, particularly given how hard we worked to make the group stage, to prove that we were worthy of the place UEFA had granted us to defend our title.

Because we were in the competition by special dispensation, when the group draw was made in Monte Carlo at the end of August, unkind fate granted not one, but two reunions with our old friends from Chelsea, as well as fixtures with Real Betis and Anderlecht.

It was hardly an easy group, but we were confident: after all, hours after the draw was made, we beat CSKA Moscow to lift the European Super Cup in Monaco's Stade Louis II, a stadium built on top of a car park and, because of that, one of the most difficult pitches in Europe. It was a close game: Cissé equalised in the eighty-second minute against a very good team, and only two goals in extra time ensured a second trophy and yet more celebrations. We knew we were good enough to reach the last sixteen.

That was the main difference that winning the Champions League had wrought. The atmosphere at the club had changed. There was a sense of progress, that we were moving forwards. Things were changing: players, methods, ideas. Everyone at Melwood, and all of the fans, knew we were going in the right direction.

The previous year, when we had drawn Bayer Leverkusen or Juventus, the assumption on the part of our opponents had been that we made for welcome guests. Yes, we were Liverpool, with all of the history and legend that that name evokes, but we were not as strong as the great sides of the past. Teams did not fear us. It would take time, but that was starting to change. The new players helped, of course, and the fact that we were getting better all the time on the pitch, in the Premier League and in the Champions League. The European Cup that stood, gleaming, at Melwood, an inspiring sight to meet you every morning, did not hurt either.

Our first game of the group stage was a trip to Seville to play Betis in the deafening, intimidating Benito Villamarin. It is one of the most impressive, raucous grounds in Spain, but we coped very well. We were two goals up within fourteen minutes, thanks to Florent

Sinama-Pongolle and Luis Garciá, but the real star of the show was Crouch.

He had a difficult start to his Liverpool career. It was not until December that he would score his first goal – a wait of nineteen games. He was criticised a lot, derided from the outside, told that he was not good enough. As that drought continued, in every press conference I had to defend his contribution, reaffirm my faith. Even without goals, though, there was no doubt he was making an impact. Among the squad, he was a popular figure, and against opponents, an unwelcome sight. After that game, Juanito, Betis's Spanish international defender, told one of his team-mates, a player I knew, that he had never encountered anything like Crouch before. One of the best defenders in Europe at the time admitted that he, and the rest of the Betis side, had no idea how to play against someone so tall and with such a fine touch.

Our second game, against Chelsea, did not have nearly so much drama as the second leg of the semi-final. It was very tight, with not many chances, and again we could close them down by playing very compact. Just a few days later, they would beat us 4–1 at Anfield in the Premier League, but in Europe, we could manage the game against them much better.

When we played them at Stamford Bridge, in the final game of the group, the same score-line – in the same type of game – ensured that we finished top. We had drawn with Betis at home, 0–0, too, but wins at home and away against Anderlecht saw us through. They were a strong team as well, but the difficulty faced by sides from countries like Belgium is that they do not have the intensity of competition in their domestic league that they encounter in European tournaments. It is hard for them to raise their levels.

The phone call came from the other side of the world on a Thursday night in the middle of December.

I had been expecting it, dreading it, for months. We knew my father was ill. We knew it was serious. He had undergone a heart operation a few weeks previously and it had left him weak, a shell of the man he once was. He had always been a strong man, with the body of an athlete. He was always in the gym. He was big, powerful. And yet the last time I had seen him, in hospital in Madrid, he had looked so frail, so fragile. The doctors said his heart was operating at just a third of its capacity. They said it was only a matter of time. We knew it was coming, but at these desperate, despairing times, such things are of no consolation.

When that phone call came, when the worst happened and he passed away, I was in Tokyo, preparing for the Club World Championship final with Sao Paulo, the South American champions, in less than forty-eight hours. In Spain, unlike in England, the custom is to hold the funeral almost immediately: rather than wait a week or so, it will often happen the next day, or two days later. I checked for flights, but the distance meant it was not possible to be back with my family in time to attend the funeral. I had no choice. I would not be able to be with them as we said goodbye to my father. It was hard to focus on football. It was hard to focus on anything, in truth. It would be too much to say that his death was a shock – he had been ill for so long that we knew it would happen soon – but I would have loved to have been able to be with my family. I was bitterly disappointed.

All I could do was wait, prepare to play Sao Paulo and then fly back. We had arrived in Japan in plenty of time for the tournament – going so far, to such different conditions, it is impossible to train normally, so we needed the chance to adapt a bit. It worked: we had beaten Deportivo Saprissa in the semi-final, 3–0, to set up the final against the Brazilian team. In between those games, I was told about my father.

Work, I suppose, was an escape. This was a competition Liverpool had never won before, and I was determined, in the circumstances, to change that. We did everything we could. We hit the bar twice, through Luis Garciá and Harry Kewell. We controlled possession completely – no easy feat against a Brazilian team, who are normally so good with the ball. Diego Lugano, their captain, should have been sent off for tripping up Steven as he bore down on goal. He was only shown a yellow card by Benito Archundia Tellez, the Mexican referee.

We had seventeen corners. Rogerio Ceni, their goalkeeper, saved shot after shot. Even when he couldn't, the linesman rescued them. Luis, Sami Hyypia and Sinama all saw goals ruled out for offside in the second half. A referee I know joked to me after the game that you should always give the third one, just to even things out. We received no such good luck. They scored midway through the first half, and we simply could not find a legal equaliser. I introduced Crouch, who had got two against Saprissa, late on; there was no reason to do so beforehand, because I could not fault the effort of any of the players. We were by far the better team, but that would count for nothing when the final whistle blew. We would not be champions of the world.

The next morning, or what seemed like the next morning, I found myself in Málaga Airport at 6 a.m., disorientated by the time difference, bleary-eyed from lack of sleep. It was eerily quiet. It seemed to me that there was nobody else there, that the airport was empty. I had taken the first flight I could from Tokyo after the final. I was alone. All I could do was wait. Wait to catch my connecting flight, wait to be back in Madrid, wait to see my mother again, and the rest of my family, to talk with them and mourn with them. Wait to attend a final ceremony for my father. Wait to say my final goodbye.

The Champions League draw, made before we travelled to Japan, had paired us with Benfica, with Simao. Failing to sign a player is always a blow: it is impossible to say, of course, but there is always the lingering question of how differently our season might have played out if we had managed to sign this player or that. Occasionally, though, it has a much more direct impact.

Part of our preparation for every game is analysing the opposition's set pieces. My video analysis team, based in their little room at Melwood, surrounded by monitors, will watch the last three or four fixtures of every team we play. Telling our defenders what they should watch out for from corners and free kicks will always form part of the team talk; we might also provide them with a DVD, too, if requested, so they can become familiar with what they will have to expect.

The build-up to that game with Benfica was no different. We had noticed from the clips that they had a clever move which culminated in Luisao, the tall Brazilian central defender, pulling away to the back post.

In that first leg, in the Stadium of Light, we were ready for it. We knew how to counter it. Football's margins are so fine, though, that all the preparation in the world can be undone by just one mistake. Sami Hyypia slipped. He would have cleared the cross Luisao headed in. We travelled back to Merseyside deflated and defeated, and with Momo Sissoko expected to be absent for some time after he suffered a horrific injury to his right eye. Beto, the central midfielder, caught him with a boot to his face and he had to be stretchered off and be taken straight to hospital. A specialist examined him. It looked very serious. At one point, he was told he might never regain his sight. It was a huge relief when later scans showed he would fully recover.

We would, however, have Steven back, a tremendous boost. He had only appeared as a late substitute in Lisbon because he had felt ill the previous night, and it was not until half-time that he felt well enough to play. And we would have Anfield, too, confident that another campaign of glory was underway, brimming with certainty that Benfica would be our first victims on the long road to Paris, where we would once again assume our rightful position as champions of Europe.

It was not to be. It would work out quite differently. John Arne Riise had returned with a sickness from Norway's trip to Senegal the previous week. Sami was injured playing for Finland in the same international break and would not recover in time. We had to reshape our defence, change our formation, drafting in Stephen Warnock at left-back and bringing Djimi Traore into the centre. It disrupted our preparation. We did not yet have a squad that could cope with injuries and absences.

With ten minutes to go in the first half, Warnock slipped as he tried to clear the ball midway inside our half. Benfica picked up the ball. Traore moved out to try to close the ball down, but was deceived by a twist of his opponent's hips. Steve Finnan and Jamie Carragher too. Pepe could do nothing as he watched the most picture-perfect, curling shot swerve beyond him. We had conceded an away goal. We needed three to progress. The scorer, needless to say, was Simao.

It seemed to deflate the players, the ground. We tried to change things around – throwing on Djibril Cissé, in the hope that his pace might stretch Benfica's static defence, introducing Robbie Fowler, returned to the club that January, to see if his experience and his instincts might give us hope. It was not to be. Late on, as we poured forward in vain, our visitors caught us on the break. Fabrizio Miccoli, with an overhead kick, put us out of Europe. All that work, all those games in the long, hot days of summer had been wasted. We had lost our crown.

It was a curious year, my second at Liverpool. We made enormous strides in the Premier League, finishing an impressive third behind Chelsea and Manchester United, with eighty-two points, the highest total the club had managed since 1989.

Our rivals now considered us a serious threat. When we beat Chelsea at Old Trafford in the FA Cup semi-final that year, with a goal from Luis Garciá over which there were absolutely no doubts, there was no courteous, cordial conversation with José afterwards, as there would have been previously. I saw him as I was talking to Rick after the game, but we did not exchange a word. I could not have asked for any more proof that he was starting to believe we posed a genuine threat to his ambitions, both at home and, of course, abroad.

That run to the FA Cup final offered proof too, I think, that we had fulfilled that promise made to Steven on the torn turf of the Ataturk, with sweat pouring down his back and a smile lighting up his face, to make him the best midfielder in the world. He scored more goals that season than he had in any year of his career, although my initial decision to play him on the right-hand side of midfield had been met with criticism.

He gave us wonderful balance there, though, and it would only be when we needed his precision, his power as a second striker, in order to get the best out of Fernando Torres, that we would find a better place for him. Quite how well he had played that season would be proved at the FA Cup final in Cardiff. He had come a long way from those frenetic days in July, when it looked like we would lose our captain, and he would lose his club.

Steven dragged us back from two goals down against West Ham on a burning hot day and then, at the very last, produced a wonderful strike to take the game to extra time. Once again, we would draw a final 3–3. Once again, we would be thankful to our goalkeeper – and the expert preparation of José Manuel Ochotorena – in a penalty shootout. Once again, Steven would end the season lifting a trophy, fireworks exploding behind him, confetti fluttering into the air. Our failure in Europe, on the other hand, that defeat to Benfica, showed we had to improve.

We had got better in the league, and winning the FA Cup ensured that the club finished the season feeling happy, jubilant. But there was still much work to be done if we were to be able to compete both in the Premier League and the Champions League; we needed a stronger squad, and we needed to learn from our experiences. We might have fallen early in Europe this year, but we would be back. And we would not make the same mistakes again.

3

Season 2006–07
The Road to Athens

THERE WAS LITTLE ROOM FOR PHOTOS IN MY OFFICE AT Melwood. One sat on my desk, a picture of a banner I had noticed flying on the Kop early on in my time at Liverpool, the words daubed in white on a red background. 'Rafa the Gaffa,' it read.

Another, an image of youth team products David Raven, Stephen Warnock and Darren Potter celebrating our Carling Cup semi-final win against Tottenham in my first season, hung on the wall. There was no other decoration, beyond a rugby ball signed by the St Helens team and, set on a shelf, a miniature European Cup. This was a place of work.

There were just a few books, all to do with football or physical education, the subject I studied at university and a life-long interest of mine, offering information on ways to train and on fitness. I had a couple of volumes of proverbs, famous quotes and inspirational sayings, but my hours were so long that I rarely had time to read anything that was not to do with work.

My desk, L-shaped, sat towards the back of the room. It boasted all the paraphernalia of any modern office, I suppose: a flat-screen computer monitor and keyboard, a printer, my laptop and several folders full of information on players and training sessions.

Every morning, a member of staff would lay out copies of press cuttings for me to read, mentions of Liverpool in that day's papers. I would leaf through them in the morning, before using the reverse sides to make notes during meetings or while on the phone.

An adjoining door, in a light wood, led to the office of my secretary. In front of my desk sat a modern, dark leather sofa, two chairs and a small, glass coffee table, an area where I would talk to members of staff, players or guests.

Light poured in through an enormous window on the back wall, offering a full view of all of our green training pitches and the suburban roofs just visible through the trees beyond. It was a spacious, if not luxurious, room. The view across the pitches, complete with players going through warm-up exercises or practising some aspect of play, was impressive.

It was quite another sight, though, that first-time visitors often found most remarkable. Perhaps not one quite so awe-inspiring as the European Cup, ours to keep after our fifth victory in the competition in Istanbul, encased in Perspex and mounted on a plinth in Melwood's slate-tiled main reception, but certainly something to make the walk up the wooden staircase, past the players' canteen and to my door worthwhile.

Stretching several metres across the wall on the right-hand side of my office stood shelves and shelves of DVDs. Hundreds upon hundreds of hours of footage, all neatly categorised, organised and numbered, so that, after consulting a database on my computer, I could find any film I needed quickly and easily. Aside from my coaching staff, this was my most valuable resource as I attempted to prepare Liverpool's players throughout the season: not just a record of all the games I had managed and training sessions I had overseen in my career, but an extensive library of football around the world.

Some of the DVDs contain recordings of games from my days as a youth coach at Real Madrid's Castilla side. Some of them have footage from Tenerife and Extremadura, and I have film of all of my games at Valencia too. There are plenty which have been compiled on opponents, on specific players we would have to face and on others who we might have liked to sign.

Then there are the discs which contain games from leagues from every corner of the globe, not just matches in Spain and Italy, but across Europe, from South America and from Africa too. There are DVDs that were prepared with specific players in mind, to showcase a certain aspect of the game. There are some that were prepared for Jamie Carragher, for example, on how my side at Valencia defended. We would show our players certain clips to illustrate how we wanted them to play, what we wanted them to do. In later years, as the ideas the coaching staff had introduced sank in and we improved, more and more of the clips we used were not of Real Madrid or

Valencia, but of Liverpool. Seeing themselves excelling in action often gave players more confidence, more motivation, and a clearer idea of their responsibilities and roles.

The DVD library did not end in my office. In the basement of my home there are all the reports from my games with Castilla, notes from my time in charge of Real Madrid's youth teams, training schedules from Tenerife and lists of all the systems I used at Extremadura and Valencia, complete with detailed analyses of how they worked. There are printouts from sessions planned on a Commodore 64 and a ZX Spectrum. This has been my system for nearly thirty years. Montse, needless to say, does not quite understand why I keep everything, but you never know when it will be relevant.

Quite how far back everything goes is best illustrated by the attic of my parents' home in Madrid. There, not only are there yet more DVDs of yet more games and yet more players, but there are videos from the early part of my career, and some Betamax cassettes too. I even have magazines and notes from my university course. All of it is cross-referenced, given a number and a location, so that I can access it on my computer whenever necessary.

This is not limited simply to games I have been involved in, players I might want to sign or potential recruits, though. There is abundant footage of past teams that I admire greatly. They can be useful when illustrating to an individual or to your squad how something should be done, what you would like them to do in any given circumstance.

Some of these examples are selected for their attacking flair. I have DVDs and videos of Johan Cruyff's Barcelona, the Dream Team he created at the Nou Camp in the early 1990s, of Romario and Pep Guardiola and Hristo Stoichkov, to show our players how wingers and strikers should move, how to build attacks, how to infuse their play with creativity and verve. There are plenty of things a team as good as that can teach players.

But there was another side that I had always admired too, for the way they pressed the ball, for the organisation of their defence, for their ability to play quickly, on the break, for their system and their approach.

On countless occasions, as we tried to illustrate our ideas to Liverpool's players, as we tried to give them an impression of what our vision was, Arrigo Sacchi's AC Milan, the side that dominated the world in the late 1980s, provided the perfect example.

Milan has played a special role in my career. That team of Ruud Gullit and Marco van Basten was one which caught my eye and fired my imagination as a young coach. I spent a few days with Fabio Capello at Milanello, trying to learn from one of the most successful managers of the modern era, and of course the club would later be assured a unique place in Liverpool's history – and my memories – after Istanbul.

Our encounters were not yet at an end.

As we reached the end of my third season at Liverpool, we would have picked our way past the heirs of the Dream Team, the modern Barcelona of Ronaldinho and Lionel Messi and Xavi, and Milan would loom large once more. Not on the screen this time, but life-size.

* * *

Just as we would for a Champions League final, we prepared a comprehensive dossier on our first opponents in the competition that season, the Israeli champions Maccabi Haifa. Those qualifying ties in early August, often held before the league season has even started, are always seen by outside observers as a foregone conclusion. In fact, they can be very dangerous.

It would be unprofessional to take any team or any game lightly, of course, but particularly these matches. Firstly, your opponents tend to be technically very able sides that are usually further along in their physical preparation for the season.

Secondly, against a team such as Liverpool, it is a massive occasion for them, and one they do not intend to spurn. When we had to play a qualifying tie before reaching the group stage, very rarely did we find it a simple affair.

Against Maccabi, things were even more complicated than normal.

We had several players to assimilate into our team that season: Mark González had joined us, a year after he had been signed, following a loan spell at Real Sociedad, and we had brought in Craig Bellamy from Blackburn, Jermaine Pennant to provide width and Fabio Aurelio, who I knew from our time together at Valencia. Just a few days after our first leg with the Israeli team, we would sign Dirk Kuyt too.

We had found ourselves in a difficult position that summer: we wanted more width on the right, and we also wanted to sign a striker. One option whom I had been alerted to was Daniel Alves, the Brazilian right-back, who was available from Sevilla. We had been tracking him since his early days in South America and we knew he was a very good player. We only had funds, though, for one purchase. We needed a striker and, with money limited, it was better to fill that slot than sign a full-back to play as a winger. We signed Kuyt.

More seriously, the political situation in Israel – where the north of the country was considered too dangerous to travel to, thanks to the war with Hezbollah in Lebanon – meant we would have to play the second leg not in Haifa, but on neutral territory. Both Austria and Holland were discussed before UEFA elected to stage the game in the Ukraine.

Regardless, we knew we would need a lead to take into that match in Kiev. To do that, we would need to know what to expect. Teams like Maccabi are much harder to find information on than Italian or Spanish sides. They are not exactly on television regularly and the players are not as familiar.

We had our scout analyse three or four games, as usual, but we had to dig deeper. I spoke to a number of people who worked with Yossi Benayoun – at that stage not yet our player, but the captain of the Israeli national side – to find out what to expect, as my analysis department got to work on assessing their style of play from DVDs.

All of that information is then compiled into a dossier. For a game like that, it would run to perhaps thirty pages, maybe more. Everything we could possibly want to know is included: details of every player, their strengths and weaknesses, the shape of the team, how they change their formation during the game according to certain circumstances, how they attack, how they defend, their speed on the counter-attack, who takes the penalties and the set pieces, if any of the side have special characteristics in their play. Nothing is missed out. The briefing we give to the players is boiled down to just fifteen or twenty minutes, but it includes anything and everything they might need to know, even for a game conventional wisdom dictates will be easy.

In the event, it was anything but. In the first leg at Anfield, Maccabi showed us that they were quick and ruthless on the counter-attack, taking the lead through Gustavo Boccoli, before Bellamy, starting his first game for the club he had supported as a boy, equalised. It was not until González scored at the Anfield Road end, in the eighty-eighth minute, that we had even the slenderest lead.

The away leg was just as difficult. There was a strange, muted atmosphere in Kiev. Both teams were a long way from home, and few fans had made the trip. Maccabi were deeply unhappy at being forced to play the game they should have hosted not just on foreign soil, but in the Ukraine in particular, and had made no secret of their anger, at Liverpool and at UEFA.

For all their energy and intensity – and even though Steven Gerrard had fallen sick before the game – we should have secured our place in the group stage in the first half in that quiet, empty stadium, but Maccabi's goalkeeper made a succession of excellent saves. Only when Peter Crouch scored ten minutes after the break did we begin to breathe more easily. Even that did not last long: Maccabi drew level on the night through Roberto Colautti, and Pepe Reina saved from him in the last few minutes to avoid extra time. It was a tense, nervous night.

Thankfully, our experience in the group that year was less fraught. We had been drawn with Bordeaux of France, the Dutch team PSV Eindhoven and Galatasaray, the Turkish champions. Each would pose their own, unique problems, but we were well equipped to qualify. In the end, we would travel to Istanbul for our final game already sure of our place in the last sixteen.

It is fair to say that teams from different nations tend to have distinct characteristics. Dutch players, for example, are taught from a young age to mark man-to-man, not just from set pieces, but in open play. As different ideas are brought into Holland, things are changing, but as a rule, they will follow players. That creates space for their opponents, who know that making certain movements will drag their players out of position, ruining their team's shape. By exploiting that space, it is possible to find opportunities. We played well in our opening group game in Eindhoven, but could not take the chances we created and were held to a goalless draw. We would have rather more luck in the return fixture at Anfield.

Turkish teams, generally speaking, have an abundance of natural ability, with technically excellent players, but tactically they are not as disciplined or alert as we were that season. The key to such teams is maintaining your defensive solidity and harrying their back-line. By playing at a high tempo, pushing their defence back and not allowing them time to play, it is possible to force them into errors.

We did exactly that in our second group game, when Galatasaray visited Anfield. After an hour, we were leading 3–0 and seemed to have victory secured.

Even then, in the Champions League, it is crucial to retain discipline and focus. Umit Karan, the Turkish team's striker, scored twice in five minutes to set up a more nerve-wracking finale than we expected. They could not, though, find an equaliser.

In my experience of French teams, the most important aspect is controlling the two or three players with tremendous pace and ability who serve as their most dangerous and most effective creative outlets. Ricardo Gomes's Bordeaux was no different.

That game also posed the problem of a very poor pitch at the Stade Chaban-Delmas, which had also proved troublesome to me when my Valencia side played there several years before. By the time I returned with Liverpool, I was in charge of a confident and experienced European side, more than capable of overcoming that sort of difficulty, as well as keeping the likes of Rio Mavuba and Johan Micoud quiet. We managed the game well and won 1–0 in France, thanks to Crouch, and beat Gomes's team 3–0 at Anfield.

A 2–0 win against PSV in our penultimate game in the group meant we could return to Istanbul for the first time since 25 May 2005 without any pressure at all: we would finish first regardless of the result, and so knew we would have the advantage of playing the first leg of our last sixteen tie away from home.

That does not mean, though, that I was not disappointed to lose that final group game.

I had chosen to send out a side full of players who had not been given too many first-team opportunities that season, in an attempt to rotate the squad a little, making sure every single member of our team retained their competitive edge.

Danny Guthrie, Lee Peltier and Gabriel Paletta all started that match, while Miki Roqué came on for the last few minutes. As for strikers, we started with Robbie Fowler and Bellamy, but too often they both drifted into the left-hand channel. Both would move out of the box to pick up the ball, leaving themselves with no options once they had received it. Our movement was not good enough, and we paid the price: a narrow 3–2 defeat.

If we needed any reminder at all that the Champions League does not afford a team so much as a single error, it came in the draw for the last sixteen of the competition, held in Nyon a few days later. We were paired with the reigning champions, Barcelona, home of the best player in the world at the time – Ronaldinho – and the young Argentine widely viewed as the heir to that title, Messi.

Managed by Frank Rijkaard, the Spanish side had won the tournament the previous season with victory over Arsenal in the final and were seen as overwhelming favourites to become the first team to retain the trophy since its rebirth as the Champions League. No wonder they were confident.

'It will be a meeting between the last two champions, so it will be an extraordinary tie,' said Barcelona's president, Joan Laporta, comments I saw him make on television in my office. 'I am happy with the draw. Liverpool are a team that I had a preference to face at this stage. They play very physical football and have players we know very well, like Luis Garciá and Xabi Alonso. Let's not forget that we are the team to beat this season.'

It is very easy to have 'a preference' to face a team when the game will not be held for three months. I was confident that we would get better as the season progressed, both at home and abroad.

Maybe it was the best draw for Barcelona in December. By February, perhaps Laporta's view would be somewhat different.

21 February 2007: Barcelona 1–2 Liverpool

Barcelona: Valdés; Belletti, Márquez, Puyol, Zambrotta; Xavi (Giuly, 65), Thiago Motta (Iniesta, 64), Deco; Messi, Saviola (Gudjohnsen, 82), Ronaldinho
Liverpool: Reina; Finnan, Carragher, Agger, Arbeloa; Gerrard, Sissoko (Zenden, 84), Alonso, Riise; Bellamy (Pennant, 80), Kuyt (Crouch, 90)

It was 2 a.m. when the phone in my hotel room rang, startling me from my sleep.

'Señor Benítez,' the voice said, 'you had better come downstairs.'

We had travelled to the Vale do Lobo resort in the Algarve area of Portugal a few days previously, for a mid-season team break in warmer weather. The idea was to give the players a chance to relax, to spend some time together and to do some training sessions the week prior to the first leg of our last sixteen tie with Barcelona.

On the Thursday night of our trip, we had relaxed the players' curfew a little, until midnight, to allow them to go for a couple of drinks at a bar called Monty's, in the town near to where we were staying. The whole squad had gone, piling into two minibuses, while the coaching staff enjoyed a quiet dinner and an early night.

It seemed there had been an argument when John Arne Riise refused to take part in a karaoke session. Bellamy had taken this as a sign that his Norwegian team-mate was not entering into the spirit of things. The two had exchanged words in the bar, and by the time they returned to the hotel, resentment was still simmering. Bellamy, incensed, had gone to his room and retrieved a golf club, before threatening Riise, striking him on the leg. The noise of the argument was enough to alert the hotel staff, who told the manager. It was his voice on the other end of that phone in the early hours of the morning. I was forced to walk from the hotel, where the staff were staying, to the players' accommodation, in a group of bungalows in the resort's grounds.

The dead of night was not the time to sort the argument out, to find out who had done what. I sent Riise back to his room, which he was sharing with Daniel Agger, and Bellamy back to his, with Steve Finnan. I left them in no doubt that I did not wish to receive another phone call that night or any other. This was hardly the sort of preparation we needed before arguably the biggest game of our season and certainly one of the most difficult matches any team could face.

The next morning, I called two meetings. The first, with Bellamy and Riise, attempted to get to the bottom of what, exactly, had happened.

When we signed him the previous summer, we knew Bellamy had enjoyed a reputation for being very strong-minded earlier in his career, but we had held a number of open and honest conversations with him while the deal was being done to bring him from Blackburn, and we were very impressed with his attitude. Those talks were really positive: he made it clear that Liverpool held a special place in his heart and that he would not waste his opportunity. I was confident he was sincere: he is a good professional, he is very talented, very competitive, and he was a very good player for us.

That morning, I made it clear to both of them that we could not let whatever had happened the previous night derail us from our main objective that season.

'We have to move on,' I said. 'We cannot have this problem before such an important match. It is over now. We have to focus on Barcelona, not these problems. We must move forward.' Both players would be punished for the events of that night, but they were willing to put the incident behind them and to focus on what was best for the team.

The second meeting was for the whole squad, to emphasise what their responsibilities to the club were, what was expected of them, and to remind them why we were in Portugal in the first place. In five days' time, we would be playing Barcelona, the best team in the world, and we would have to be fully focused on the task in hand if we were to stand any chance of beating them.

Even a side containing such talent as Ronaldinho, Deco, Xavi, Andres Iniesta and Messi can be beaten if you have a plan. As we flew to Catalunya, the week after our unexpectedly feisty trip to the Algarve, I was confident we did.

It seems strange now, but playing Barcelona then was not simply a matter of doing anything we could to stop Messi. We were just as concerned with how to cope with Ronaldinho. The Brazilian played on the left wing, nominally, but would drift inside, occupying space between the lines.

That would create a problem for Steve Finnan, our right-back. If he tracked Ronaldinho, he would leave space for Barcelona's left-back, Gianluca Zambrotta, to exploit. The threat of Barcelona's number ten, though, was more important. I instructed Finnan to follow his man, to push him, not to allow him a moment to play the sort of penetrating pass which could cut a defence apart in a second.

On the opposite side, we would play Alvaro Arbeloa, signed as recently as January from Deportivo La Coruña, against Messi. It would be Arbeloa's first appearance for Liverpool. His opponent was just a teenager, not yet talked about as one of the finest players in history, but it was still one of the more intimidating debuts in world football.

Arbeloa is not the sort of player to get scared, though, and he was confident he could do what was being asked of him. Besides, a manager does not simply come up with an idea and then tell his players about it an hour or so before the game. In Portugal, and upon our return to Melwood, we worked extensively on what we hoped Arbeloa would do.

The principle was relatively simple. Messi, playing wide on the right, favoured cutting inside on his left foot. By playing Arbeloa, naturally right-footed, at left-back, we would be able to prevent him embarking on those dangerous, slaloming runs. Arbeloa would have to stick close to his man too, not allowing him to breathe. If Messi has time to turn, he can inflict substantial damage. We had to be on top of him all the time.

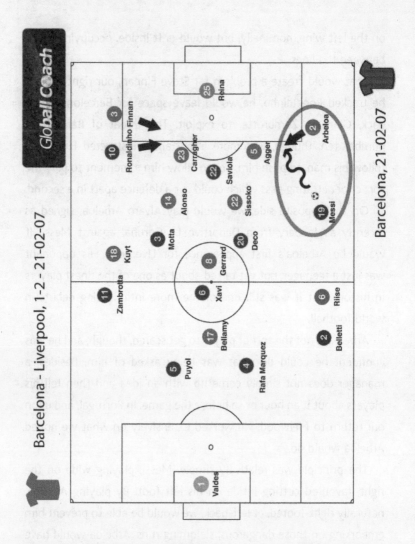

It was on the flanks that Barcelona were most threatening. On one side, Alvaro Arbeloa would play at left-back, tasked with stifling the runs of Lionel Messi. There are not many tougher debuts in world football. On the other, Steve Finnan was told not to allow Ronaldinho space to cut inside.

We drilled our new, makeshift left-back extensively in the days before the game. We prepared DVDs for him, so he knew Messi's movements. In training, we played him at left-back, against a left-footed player, to get him used to the job he would have to do in Barcelona.

And we prepared the rest of the team, particularly our defenders, not to use Arbeloa too much when we had possession. The danger of playing a right-footed full-back at left-back is that he has to turn his body inside to play the ball, which cuts off his options and slows down counter-attacks. It was crucial that we did not give him too much of the ball.

That Barcelona team had more than just two threats, of course. Their midfield, marshalled by Thiago Motta, could play short, quick passes to pick their opponents apart. Their wide players, by drifting inside, tried to pull the defence out of shape to create space for Deco, running forward from deep, to exploit. We would have to work incredibly hard, remain compact and narrow at all times, to keep them at bay. That was the crux of my team talk before the game.

We had to make our lateral movements – when the right-sided centre-back moves across to support the right-back, the left-sided centre-back moves across to cover, and the left-back moves across in unison, and vice versa – extremely quickly, without hesitation or doubt. We had to move seamlessly as a unit.

We knew they would interchange positions at will, an intrinsic part of that style that has now become so famous, and we told the players that Barcelona would press the ball early and high up the pitch. Much of their game is based around regaining the ball as close to the opposition's goal as possible.

And we wanted to allow Carles Puyol, their captain, to have the ball. He was playing as a left-sided centre-back, despite being right-footed. If we could cut off his options for a pass, we would be able to stifle a lot of Barcelona's attacks.

We did not travel without a plan to score, though. They did not have too many players looking to run in behind our defence, so we too could press the ball high up the pitch, trying to force them into a mistake.

'We need intensity at the back,' I said. 'And determination when we counter-attack. Attack the wide areas. Their full-backs will go forward. But most important is that we work for each other, as a team.'

A team of Barcelona's quality, though, will always be dangerous. That night at the Nou Camp is one of my proudest as a manager, but though we started well, still there were things we needed to do better.

We did not press Xavi and Thiago Motta with enough intensity in the first half. Daniel Agger needed to be tighter to Javier Saviola – playing instead of Samuel Eto'o – who on two or three occasions threatened to wriggle clear. Craig Bellamy, playing just behind Dirk Kuyt, with Steven Gerrard on the right flank, needed to recover more quickly. Each one only a slight failing, demanding just a little improvement. But at Barcelona there is no room for error.

Deco, bursting forwards from midfield into the right-hand side of our penalty area, headed in a cross from Zambrotta midway through the first half.

It is easy to think that a manager starts to fear the worst when, twenty-five minutes into a game at the Nou Camp, his team fall a goal behind. But I do not find myself anxious, worrying about what might happen, in those situations. You are so focused on thinking about a solution that no other thoughts enter your mind.

We needed to keep the ball better. Barcelona were pressing Xabi Alonso, closing him down quickly, but leaving Jamie Carragher free, allowing him possession. Arbeloa, when not shackling Messi, could go forward a little more. It was important for Pepe Reina to steer his goal kicks away from Motta, a towering presence in their midfield, who would drop off to win each and every header if we played the ball long.

Every observation was conveyed to the team. No sense of panic, simply adjustments. We got our reward just before half-time, Finnan crossing and Bellamy's header at the far post being carried just over the line by Víctor Valdés, the Barcelona goalkeeper. Even had the goal not been allowed to stand, Kuyt had followed up and converted the rebound as Bellamy celebrated his strike by miming the swing of a golf club.

Better was to come. We made a few further tweaks at half-time – we had to stop their full-backs crossing the ball earlier, we needed to break more quickly on the counter-attack – but the system was working. It is important not to change too much if things are going well. It is all too easy to make an alteration and find that you have lost control of the game.

In that second half, we pushed Barcelona back. We had to remain attentive, but Kuyt might have scored another away goal before

Riise did, the Norwegian bursting forward from the left wing to fire the ball into the roof of the net with his weaker right foot. Of course, it is just the way that football works that it was Bellamy – the man with whom he had argued so fiercely just a week before – who set him up. I was pleased. Both were focused completely on the team, not allowing personal issues to cloud their work, just as I had asked of them.

Taking that lead back to Anfield would be crucial. I sent on Boudewijn Zenden, a former Barcelona player, and switched to five in midfield in an attempt to close the game out, tasking Kuyt with playing as a lone striker. Jermaine Pennant came on to give us fresh legs on the counter-attack and, in injury time, Crouch, to hold the ball better. Still, even at the last, we might have lost our famous win, as Deco's free kick clattered against the post, but we survived, and deservedly so.

As our fans, high up in the towering Nou Camp, sang the anthem to commemorate another of Europe's great cathedrals conquered, we could reflect that our plan, so carefully honed on the training pitch and so painstakingly perfected, had worked to a tee. Perhaps we weren't such ideal opponents for Barcelona, after all.

It could not have been easy for Liverpool's new owners to grasp what was going on as they sat, red and white scarves draped around their necks, in Anfield's directors' box two weeks later, listening to the Kop in full voice, bellowing 'You'll Never Walk Alone'. All around them, officials and dignitaries, wives and girlfriends, friends and family were embracing, celebrating yet another famous European victory. On the pitch, the players exchanged high-fives and hugs.

And yet, they must have thought on the night we had lost, thanks to a late goal from Eidur Gudjohnsen. And in the tie, we had drawn 2–2 with Barcelona on aggregate. Why was everyone so happy? Tom Hicks and George Gillett, for the first time watching the club they had bought just a few weeks previously, must have been thoroughly confused.

That night, before the game, I was taken from the dressing room to the boardroom by the outgoing owner, David Moores, to meet the two Americans who, years after Liverpool's search for new investment had begun, had spent £188 million to buy the club.

I had already been introduced to Gillett, who had tried to buy Liverpool on his own a few months previously. I had also met twice with Dubai International Capital, DIC, who for a long time looked like the most likely group to provide the club with the money it required to compete with Manchester United, Arsenal and Chelsea. John Miskelly, another potential investor, had also been introduced to me at Melwood by Rick Parry.

But that night was the first time I met Tom Hicks, who would become such a central figure to Liverpool over the next three years. It may have been the first night anyone had met him, this tall Texan who had emerged only at the last minute to invest in the club.

I have to admit that both Gillett and Hicks made the right impression, both that night – when our meeting was only brief – and during the following weeks, when we spoke more about their plans for the club. Right from their very first press conference, held at Melwood, they were making the right noises, and it seemed as though David and Rick had chosen well when they'd agreed to sell the club.

In those first few conversations, they were desperate for information on how I wanted the club to progress. We talked about the need to sign new players, my wish to see the academy revamped so that we might start bringing through more local, home-grown players, the heirs to Gerrard and Carragher, how I thought we might improve the structure of the club and, of course, their ideas for the stadium. There was no sign then, in those first few months, of what was to come.

No doubt seeing Liverpool eliminate the reigning European champions from the Champions League in the first game they attended helped convince them they had made a wise decision, once someone had explained the away goals rule to them.

It was a performance I was proud of too. Tactically, the first thirty minutes were among the best I ever saw Liverpool play.

We had spoken in the build-up of the need to press Barcelona relentlessly, all over the pitch, right from the very first whistle. We had to make sure they could not build up any sort of momentum.

And we knew, too, that the wide areas would be crucial to our hopes of adding to our lead and killing off the tie.

Rijkaard set his side up in a 3–4–3 formation, with Oleguer Presas, Puyol and Lilian Thuram in his defensive line. On both wings, we would have the opportunity to find space. John Arne Riise and Steven Gerrard – playing wide on the right, as he had in the Nou Camp – would have abundant opportunities to move forward. As they attacked, though, trying to find space between the lines and playing

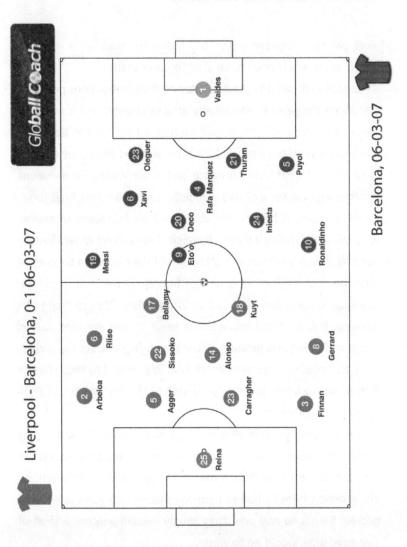

At Anfield, we instructed John Arne Riise and Steven Gerrard to exploit the space left out wide by Frank Rijkaard's 3–4–3 formation. The result was possibly the best half of football, tactically, I saw in my time at Liverpool.

wall passes – one-twos, give-and-gos – to open up Barcelona's defence, we would need to be alert to cover them.

In that first half, the players followed their instructions perfectly. Barcelona struggled to mount any attacks of note, and it was only through great good fortune that we had not settled the tie before we headed in for the interval. John Arne Riise and Momo Sissoko had both struck the bar from a distance, and Víctor Valdés, the Barcelona goalkeeper, made one or two wonderful saves from Dirk Kuyt too.

At no point did Barcelona abandon their principles, of course. Even when defending a corner, they left three strikers forward, ready for a lightning-quick counter-attack. I told the players to be wary of that threat at half-time. We needed to keep up the intensity of our pressing, to harry Barcelona out of their rhythm. We deserved to be winning, but we could not afford a lapse in concentration. Daniel Agger had to hold his position, rather than trying to track the endless runs, the intelligent movement, of Xavi. We needed to keep the ball better, not to invite pressure on ourselves by playing back to Pepe Reina, our goalkeeper.

We were not yet safe. Not by a long way. Ronaldinho hit the post early in the second half, a warning that we needed to maintain our focus. And then, with fifteen minutes to go, Eidur Gudjohnsen, on the ground where he had so narrowly missed two years previously, scored. Barcelona had one. They simply needed another and all of our good work would go to waste.

I was concerned – it would be impossible not to be – but I knew we deserved to go through and I trusted my players to see the game out. We moved to a 4–5–1 formation to keep the ball better and to close down the space in midfield, and in defence we were narrow, compact, denying Barcelona the space they needed to play through balls.

As the clock ticked down and the Kop began to sing – much to the confusion of the owners – I could see we were in control. We had lost on the night, and drawn on aggregate, but won another famous victory. Now the rest of Europe would be in no doubt that Liverpool were to be taken very seriously indeed. Nobody would have a preference for facing us for the remainder of the tournament.

We did not celebrate that win. There was no party organised. I fulfilled my media engagements, giving interviews to countless broadcasters and the written press in the trophy room, before having something to eat in my office. Everyone simply went home. We had not achieved anything yet. It had not even come as a surprise, although the result was certainly a shock to Ronaldinho, Messi and their team-mates, and maybe the other teams in the competition had not thought that we would get through. We'd had no such doubts. We had been confident that we would beat Barcelona. The best team in the world held no fear for us.

I have always hated to lose.

When I was thirteen or fourteen, I would spend hours during the summer playing the board game Stratego against my brother and my friends.

It is a tactical game, with the players' forces drawn up on either side of the board and a lake drawn in the middle. Each side has an army and a flag, a total of forty pieces, ranging from Marshal, the highest rank, down to Scout, the lowest. There are bombs and mines, spies and sergeants. You organise your pieces however you wish, taking care not to give your opponent any clue as to how you have set your army up.

Each player moves one piece every turn. If you land on a square occupied by a piece belonging to your opponent, a third player, the judge, rules which is the stronger piece. The loser is removed from the board.

So the Captain beats the Lieutenant, the General beats the Colonel, and the Marshal wins against everyone except the Spy. The Spy loses against everyone except the Marshal. The aim is to find your opponent's flag, or to remove so many of their pieces that they can no longer make any moves, but the genius of the game, and what makes it so interesting, is that, because the judge does not reveal which pieces have been removed, you can never be sure exactly how strong your opponent's forces are.

It is a complex, tactical game, and for a few summers, when school had finished, it was all we played.

As I say, though, I hated to lose. So, for one day and one night, I analysed the game, considering each piece, its strengths and weaknesses, how it could best be used. I wrote everything down and drew up a plan. I decided how I would play the game, what my strategy would be, and resolved to stick to it. I knew how I would move the pieces, where I would station each part of my army, the attacks I would make.

The basic principle was to toy with what my opponent expected me to do, to move the pieces in such a way that they would mistakenly assume certain characters were in certain places, and to keep some pieces back, so that you did not risk losing by finding your forces suddenly depleted. All of my work did not go to waste. My brother and my friends never beat me again.

It was the same when I went to Real Madrid, first as a player, then as a coach. It was a place that shared my loathing for defeat. To finish second was viewed as a disaster, from the first day you joined. The club had seen me as a player when I was twelve, playing for the team which won a schools' championship in Madrid, and drafted me into their youth academy. I was at Real, where losing was unacceptable, for seven years as a player, in the youth teams and the reserve side, and returned as a coach when I was twenty-six. After a while, such an attitude towards defeat becomes ingrained in you.

I remember my first game in charge of one of the club's youth teams well. It would go on to be a successful season, but that match stands out. It was my first defeat as a coach.

The game pitted us against a school from my area of Madrid, and we lost 2–1 because the club made a mistake: they told me I was only allowed a squad of fifteen players when, in fact, we were able to play sixteen. I was furious when the referee, an old colleague, told me that the rules had been changed for that season, but Real Madrid had not realised. Who knows? That extra substitute might have made all the difference.

That defeat taught me an important lesson. The fine details matter. That is a philosophy that has guided me as a coach, from youth football in Spain, to Extremadura and Tenerife, and then to Valencia and Liverpool. Take care of everything, leave nothing to chance. Take care of the small things, whether in a friendly or in a Champions League semi-final.

After plotting our way past Barcelona, the draw for the quarter-finals had paired us with PSV Eindhoven, who had qualified with us from the group stage. We managed the game extremely well in Holland, winning 3–0 and all but securing a second semi-final in three years. There was one considerable blow, though, after Peter Crouch had added to our earlier goals from Steven Gerrard and John Arne Riise: Fabio Aurelio, excellent for us throughout that season at left-back, was stretchered off with a ruptured Achilles tendon. It would rule him out not just for the return leg at Anfield – a professional 1–0 win, with Crouch again the goal-scorer – but, more seriously, for the rest of the campaign.

Fabio may not be the fastest player, but he was crucial in helping us play the ball out from defence, retain possession, and his positional awareness was superb. He was a really key player for us. Losing him was a great shame, particularly given the identity of our semi-final opponents. Chelsea, again, awaited.

By the end of that season, we were familiar foes. We had met each other fifteen times since Mourinho and I moved to England in the summer of 2004. On such occasions, things are decided by the finest margins. Who wins the looming fixture can come down to the respective quality of players at your disposal. It can also come down to who has the best plan.

We drew up an enormous file on Chelsea for our trip to London. Everything we had learned from our previous games in the Premier

League, the FA Cup, the Carling Cup and, of course, the Champions League. All of the reports of the matches, the players' statistics, an analysis of what we had done, what they had done, what had worked and what had failed. No doubt Chelsea did exactly the same – it is, after all, a problem both teams face when playing a side they know so well. It is very hard to surprise each other.

Chelsea had changed a little since our victory over them in 2005, of course. They had added Andriy Shevchenko to their squad and were playing more with two strikers to accommodate him. They would not win the Premier League that year, but they were still dangerous opponents. We needed to remain tight in defence, playing very narrow, at Stamford Bridge – where they had not lost a league game since José Mourinho took charge – and to be first to the second balls if we were to keep the tie alive ahead of the second leg at Anfield.

We did just that. It was a tight, tense game. At that time, all of our games with Chelsea fitted that description: closely fought affairs between two teams with little between them when in direct competition. Again, we selected Steven Gerrard on the right, with Xabi Alonso and Javier Mascherano, signed on loan from West Ham in January, in midfield. Bolo Zenden, a good professional, intelligent in his use of the ball and tactically very aware, played on the left. The idea was to stretch their defence with Dirk Kuyt and Craig Bellamy as strikers.

There were few chances for either side. Joe Cole put Chelsea ahead in the first half, the goal they could not score in 2005, but we controlled the match for long periods. Gerrard might have equalised after the break, but for a flying save from Petr Cech, and Pepe Reina had to make two impressive stops near the end to make sure we went to Anfield just a goal behind.

1 May 2007: Liverpool 1–0 Chelsea (Liverpool win 4–1 on penalties)

Liverpool: Reina; Finnan, Carragher, Agger, Riise; Pennant (Alonso, 78), Gerrard, Mascherano (Fowler, 118), Zenden; Kuyt, Crouch (Bellamy, 106)
Chelsea: Cech; Ferreira, Essien, Terry, A Cole; Mikel, Makelele (Geremi, 118), Lampard; J Cole (Robben, 98), Drogba, Kalou (Wright-Phillips, 107)

Before every Champions League home game, the squad would gather together in the morning at a hotel outside Liverpool. We would have lunch, a short rest in the afternoon, and a brief, final team talk before setting off for Anfield about two hours before the match.

We did not need to talk too much: the majority of the work had been done during the week at Melwood, taking players aside, going through specific training exercises, giving individuals DVDs of certain aspects of their or their opponents' play.

It is crucial that match-day routine does not change. The worst thing is for the players to be panicked. It is better for them, and for us, if they are relaxed, comfortable in their surroundings. Knowing exactly what is going on helps with their preparation.

Even during that short afternoon rest in the hotel, a manager has a role to play. I would sometimes ask that a right-back share a room

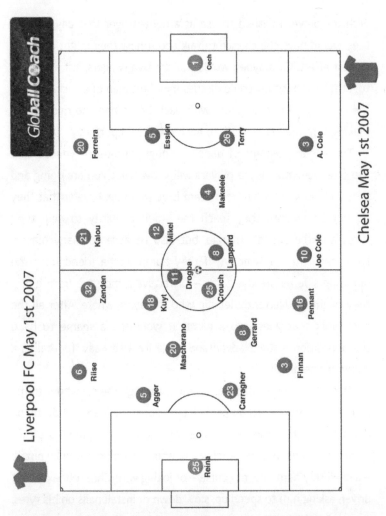

We named Bolo Zenden and Jermaine Pennant as wingers with the aim of forcing Chelsea's full-backs to concentrate on their defensive duties, preventing them from attacking. Steven Gerrard's role was to break from midfield and try to win the ball between the lines. The plan worked: we ought to have won the tie in normal time, with Petr Cech making two or three impressive saves to keep us out.

with the player I wished to use as a right-winger that day, so that they would have the chance to talk about how they might combine to best effect. Or maybe I would put the two wingers, left and right, together, so that they could discuss their best plan of attack. Perhaps the centre-backs could share with each other, and the midfielders. Making sure the players talk to each other is important.

There is an element of danger, though, because if you do that too often, eventually the players will know what you are doing and they will work out what your team is going to be. I prefer that they do not know until they reach the stadium, partly to help their focus and the squad's morale, but also because so many players know each other nowadays. If they bump into a friend from the opposing side before the game – or receive a message from him – they might inadvertently let slip who is playing where. After all the hard work that goes into a game, it would be a shame to hand the opposition a slight advantage so easily. Like I say, football is a game of fine details.

The mood on the coach, as it crawls through the rush-hour traffic in north Liverpool, accompanied by police outriders, tends to be quiet. I sit at the front, either reading and analysing reports or, if I want a moment to relax, reading a newspaper, doing a Sudoku puzzle – a devilishly hard one, of course – or joking with Chris, our excellent driver, asking him to speed up, slow down or install nails on his tyres, to get us to the ground faster.

Some of the players read notes, a few like to talk, some sit with their headphones on, listening to music and starting to concentrate on the game ahead. Each one has his own routine. The more superstitious among them will prefer to sit with the same team-mate every time, and some don't mind.

As we drove towards Anfield two hours before our second leg with Chelsea, it would not have been hard to guess the thoughts running through the players' minds.

We knew we would have the advantage of our home support, of course, the noise and the colour and the hope of 45,000 fans willing us to reach yet another Champions League final. It had startled Chelsea's players two years previously, I think, when they walked out into that cauldron of passion. We hoped for the same effect again.

The key difference this year, though, was that Chelsea had a lead to defend. We knew we would have to be as intense as we had been in 2005, in Turin, in the Nou Camp, if we were to stand a chance of reaching the final, but we would have to do more too. We would need to do something they were not expecting.

We knew set pieces would be an important chance to take Mourinho's team by surprise. A team practises a number of corner- and free-kick routines, but you do not always use the same ones every game. In fact, I have always thought it is best to leave your best, most intelligent routines for really important games.

As a manager, you tend to look two, three or maybe four games ahead. That is how many of your previous matches your opponents will be analysing, just as we do as part of our preparation. So if you have a big game coming up, you do not give everything away. You do not use all of the routines you have been working on. You leave one or two in store, so that your opponents in the most important match will not be expecting them.

Your own scouts have a role to play too. If you see from their reports of the opposition and the videos of their most recent matches that they are, for example, weak at the near post from corners, then maybe in the preceding two games, you play all of your corners to the far post, or deep into the box. Anywhere but to the near post. You save that for the team it will damage the most.

That was how we cancelled out Chelsea's advantage twenty minutes or so into our second leg. It was a free-kick routine we had been practising, but one I had not used since my Valencia side played Celtic in Spain several years before. We scored that night through Vicente. This time, it would be Daniel Agger.

The routine works by one player dropping out of the box as all the others, stationed on the edge of the penalty area, rush in. Against Chelsea, it was just as we had envisioned in training. Steven Gerrard won a foul on the left-hand side of the pitch. He took the free kick himself, playing the ball short to Agger, who had come out of the area to meet it. A low, left-footed shot which took Petr Cech by surprise. The Kop, 100 metres away at the other end of the pitch, erupted. The players embraced. Chelsea's lead was wiped out. We were level, and the storm was gathering.

We might have won that game in normal time. We had named Zenden and Jermaine Pennant as wingers, in the hope of stopping Chelsea's full-backs attacking, pushing their defensive line back and creating space for Steven Gerrard to run into between the lines. We started with just one holding midfielder, Mascherano, with Xabi Alonso on the bench.

Only a lack of good fortune stopped us finishing the game off.

Cech kicked away a header from Crouch, after a pinpoint cross from Pennant. A few moments later, Kuyt met a Riise cross, but his header cannoned off the bar. We could not find a second, the goal that would have avoided the need for extra time, and Chelsea were not able to find a way past Reina to score the away goal that would have made our task so much harder. We would have extra time.

We seemed to cope better with tiring legs and weary minds than our opponents. Kuyt had a goal ruled out for offside, an extremely tight call from the referee, Manuel Mejuto González, the same man who had overseen our victory in Istanbul. There would be no winning strike. Here, too, under the Spanish official's watchful eyes, we would see a penalty shootout.

On such occasions, we were always confident. José Manuel Ochotorena had, by then, been replaced by Xavi Valero, a well-regarded goalkeeping coach who had a close relationship with Reina, and he continued the work we had been doing to analyse and revise all of the details of our opponents' penalty kicks. Just like Jerzy Dudek in Istanbul, that night, as he walked to the Anfield Road end, Pepe was prepared.

As we were waiting for the shootout to start, though, I noticed that the people in the lower rows of the Paddock, that part of Anfield's Main Stand situated just behind the dugout, would not be able to see because of all the staff standing on the edge of the technical area.

Though the players had gathered in the centre circle, all of the coaches, doctors and physios were standing together by the substitutes' benches. It seemed that the view of those supporters in the seats nearest the touchline was blocked. There was only one thing for it. I decided I would have to sit down.

That image has become famous, almost romantic. People have suggested that maybe I was trying to spread an aura of calm or send a message to the players, but no: I simply wanted to make sure everyone in the ground could see. Knowing how much work had gone into Pepe's revision of Chelsea's penalty-takers, I was confident they would want to enjoy the shootout.

Once again, we were not short of players who wanted to step up. That should not be a surprise: our record was fantastic. We had won a European Cup and an FA Cup on penalties. There was no reason why this should be any different, with all of Anfield roaring us on.

Boudewijn Zenden, technically excellent, went first. Cech dived right, Zenden shot left. We had the lead.

Arjen Robben. Pepe Reina, a last-minute reminder of where each player was likely to go fresh in his mind, leapt rapidly to his left to meet the Dutchman's shot. Saved. Advantage Liverpool.

Xabi Alonso, right along the ground, but just out of Cech's reach. 2–0.

Frank Lampard, to a chorus of jeers from Anfield. Reina went the right way, but the shot was too powerful. 2–1.

Steven Gerrard, his name ringing around the ground. Low, to the right, stroked into the net. 3–1.

Geremi, brought on by Mourinho late on in extra time, one of his penalty specialists. To Reina's left. Saved, with the goalkeeper's trailing hand. 3–1. If we scored our next kick, we would be in Athens.

Dirk Kuyt. Low, into the corner. Scored. My staff raced onto the pitch. The players hared down to celebrate with Kuyt and Reina. All around, 45,000 people appeared to be jumping, bouncing.

I walked onto the pitch, as I always did, hoping to catch one or two of my players to pass on a little piece of advice, something that had occurred to me during the match that they could improve for the next game. It is the manager's duty always to think of what is to come, not what has just happened.

I did not get very far before Craig Bellamy put his arm around me, beaming. 'You,' he said, giving me a hug, 'are a f****** genius.' I have never seen him so happy. I am not entirely sure I have ever seen anyone so happy. Chelsea were beaten, as PSV Eindhoven and Barcelona had been. Liverpool would be in the Champions League final once again.

We did celebrate that night. Though we had no party booked, because we did not wish to invite misfortune, we had an arrangement with the owners of the Sir Thomas Hotel in Liverpool city centre that we would head there should we win the game, should our place in Athens be secured.

Again, my media duties are such that it is impossible to leave the ground much before 12.30 a.m., or maybe even as late as 1 a.m. But, the endless rounds of interviews done, I went with Montse and some family and friends to the bar, where we were greeted by the players, the staff and all of their friends, relatives and guests.

Just as I had when we celebrated beating Chelsea at the same stage two years previously, I spent the night being taught the words to Liverpool songs and posing for photos. It was a wonderful, friendly, delighted atmosphere. We knew the whole city was celebrating our success – or half of it, at least – and it was a pleasure to be able to join in, especially surrounded by so many people who had contributed to what we had achieved.

That night, I could not talk about what we would have to do to win the competition: we did not, at that stage, know who we would be facing. It could be Manchester United, our fiercest rivals, or Milan, out for revenge after Istanbul. All there was to do before we found out was enjoy the moment we had earned.

I left at around 3 a.m., with the party in full flow. It was a school night, after all, and we would have to be awake for the children the next day. We rarely woke the girls up when we came home late from a game – they would be asleep in their bedrooms, two flights of stairs up – though we would have to be careful not to wake Honey and Goofy, our spaniels. Their barking would disturb the girls. We had to be quiet when we got home.

At the Sir Thomas, I think things were less peaceful. Pako Ayesterán, my assistant, had been promised a bottle of champagne if we reached the final by Frank McParland, our joint chief scout. True to his word, Frank duly bought a bottle for Pako when they arrived at the Sir Thomas. Pako opened it, poured the entire bottle over Frank, and then asked for another one, to drink this time.

In the very early hours of the morning, Steven Gerrard was trying to get home, but was unable to flag down a taxi. I was told later that he had hitched a ride on a passing milk float, though only very briefly, before finding a cab that would take him home to bed.

In football, the fine details do matter. But so, too, does allowing your players and staff to enjoy the rewards of all their hard work.

Nights like that help everyone relax, to appreciate what they have done. Ideally, though, they would not involve milk floats.

In the stands, Steven had his hands raised to his head and a look of horror on his face. Beneath him, Dirk Kuyt was catching his breath, trying to scramble to his feet. Peter Crouch was careering round at high speed and with no way of stopping. It was a week before the Champions League final, and our centre-forward had just come within a whisker of running his strike partner over.

We had been advised to travel to the south of Spain, to La Manga, a hotel and resort near Murcia, for a few days in the build-up to our rematch with AC Milan. In Athens, late in May, our players would have to deal with the sort of ferocious heat they were not used to in the English spring, and we thought it would be a good idea to do some light training sessions in warm weather, to help them adapt.

Generally, players do not like being away from their families, holed up for days on end with only their team-mates for company. South American players, who while playing in Argentina and Brazil will often stay in a hotel for a week before matches, are used to it. But before a game of such magnitude, everyone knew it was for the best. We could leave nothing to chance.

We trained twice a day, taking care not to ask too much of the squad, with our sessions overseen by our physiologists, a group of specialists from Spain who had been recommended by Pako Ayesterán. They measured a number of aspects of the players' performance in the training sessions and controlled their diets, so they would be in peak physical condition when we got to Athens. We even used jackets lined with ice to help bring their body temperatures down. The idea was that they would wear them for a couple of minutes at half-time, cool down, and perform even better in the second half.

We knew, though, that we needed to prevent the players from becoming bored, so we agreed to let them spend an afternoon go-karting at a track near the hotel. It was as they were racing round, at speeds reaching thirty miles an hour, that Peter Crouch suddenly realised that his brakes were not working. I was standing with Kuyt by a pile of cardboard boxes at the side of the track. Crouch, fearing he would not be able to stop normally, decided to try to crash into the boxes.

He was aiming straight for Kuyt, who had to jump out of the way at the very last second. Crouch thumped into the boxes, came out of the other side and carried on round the track, waiting to get to the straight before jumping out of his kart and rolling away, thankfully unscathed. How he managed to do that, given his height and the small size of the kart, I have absolutely no idea. His knees were pointing out of the kart even before things started to go wrong.

Kuyt dusted himself down and checked he was OK. Gerrard, not involved in the race, waited anxiously to find out if we had lost either one of our forwards to one of the more preventable injuries in football: ruled out of the most important game of their careers by go-karting. Thankfully, Crouch emerged a little sheepish, but physically fine – and so, too, was Kuyt.

'We have to reduce the maximum speed,' I told the man in charge of the track. 'Can we limit the karts to twenty miles an hour?' He was happy to oblige.

I think Bolo Zenden won the day's racing, at a crawl. He might have been faster than Xabi Alonso, but suffice to say, Fernando Alonso is safe for now.

At least the facilities at La Manga were good, the players able to enjoy their preparations in comfort. When we arrived in Athens, the contrast could not have been sharper. The hotel came as a shock.

I could not believe my eyes when I first saw the rooms. The bathrooms were so small that some of our taller players, like Pepe Reina, could not even stand up in the shower. The beds were singles, not doubles, with lumpy mattresses that were so soft you sank right into them. You could lie down flat on some of them and in a minute find yourself sliding towards the floor. Crouch's legs were hanging over the end. It was simply unacceptable to ask the players to deal with these things three days before a Champions League final. It looked like a cheap hostel, not a hotel fit for finely tuned athletes.

My first thought was to find the manager, to tell him that this was unacceptable. We had sent our travel representatives out to check on the hotel the month before, but they had not been shown these rooms. Together with Rick Parry, we confronted the manager.

'This isn't good enough,' we said. 'The players cannot stay here. We either need to be given better quality rooms or we will have to go elsewhere.'

He did what he could, moving us to the more modern part of the hotel, on the opposite side of the interior garden to the ramshackle rooms we had been shown. It was better, if hardly ideal. The players' families were still thirty miles away, across Athens, and we did not have enough rooms to accommodate the staff in the new section. For a final, everything needs to be in place, to be just right. It was not an auspicious start.

The key over those two days, once we had settled into our far from luxurious surroundings, was to keep the players busy. We did not need to summon them for too many meetings, full of rousing speeches, or try to calm them down, as we had in Istanbul. Instead, we tried to maintain as much of our routine as possible.

The danger is that the players, separated from their families and bereft of normal life, grow bored. That is when the nerves can set in. So it is vital to provide them with enough activities to distract them. We watched videos of Milan from previous rounds, spoke to individual players at length about what they would need to do on the Wednesday night, and went through light training sessions. Even a simple session of stretching on the hotel terrace can help lift the tension. The players have to get changed, go to the terrace, do their exercises, then go back to their rooms, take a shower, get changed again. Before you knew it, two hours or so had been taken up and they had not been sitting in front of the television, thinking about what was to come, the moment that awaited them at the Olympic Stadium in less than forty-eight hours' time.

23 May 2007: AC Milan 2–1 Liverpool

AC Milan: Dida; Oddo, Nesta, Maldini, Jankulovski (Kaladze, 79); Gattuso, Pirlo, Ambrosini; Seedorf (Favalli, 90), Kaka; Inzaghi (Gilardino, 88)
Liverpool: Reina; Finnan (Arbeloa, 88), Carragher, Agger, Riise; Alonso, Mascherano (Crouch, 78); Pennant, Gerrard, Zenden (Kewell, 59); Kuyt

Two years minus two days since Istanbul, Steven Gerrard and Paolo Maldini walked out alongside each other again in Athens, their stride only broken by the European Cup, on a plinth by the side of the pitch. A familiar sight for both – Milan, like Liverpool, have a replica of the trophy to keep – but a gleaming prize, that night, for just one.

In Milan's team were players who had experienced that night by the Bosphorus, players who remembered what had happened the last time they played Liverpool. Dida, Maldini, Gennaro Gattuso, Andrea Pirlo, Clarence Seedorf, Kaka. Standing beside me on the touchline, the man who had watched on helplessly as what he called 'six mad minutes' cost him the Champions League trophy.

And yet, if Carlo Ancelotti's team had not changed so much on paper, this was a very different side. They now played more of a 4–2–3–1 formation, more heavily reliant on the creativity of Kaka than they had been two years previously. They played through the Brazilian almost every time they went forward. We knew, again from our extensive scouting and analysis, that the key to winning a second Champions League in two years was shutting Kaka down.

Milan were not the only team that had changed. We were now a much more confident side, far more complete, ready to stand and look Milan in the eye, to try to outplay them, not just to outthink them.

We knew their full-backs, Massimo Oddo and Marek Jankulovski, would look to provide width in attack, raiding forward at every available opportunity. That made Jermaine Pennant and Boudewijn Zenden key to our game plan. We would try to get those two running behind Milan's full-backs, getting crosses in. Dirk Kuyt, a lone striker, was tasked with pushing the central defenders back. Steven Gerrard, playing in the advanced role that he would soon make his own, would look for the second balls. Javier Mascherano and Xabi Alonso, two members of what the Kop now proclaimed 'the greatest midfield in the world', were tasked with holding, keeping an eye on Kaka's bursts through the middle.

Zenden, perhaps, seemed a strange selection. We had Mark González available too, who had much more pace than the veteran Dutchman, but Zenden had the tactical expertise we needed. He was intelligent in possession, he worked hard, covered well, and the idea was to use him until early in the second half, when I planned to unleash Harry Kewell.

A lot of Liverpool fans never got to see the best of the Australian, because of the injuries that plagued him at Anfield. But Kewell, like few others, could beat a man, he had a good shot, he had pace and he was good in the air. The word we use in Spanish is *desequilibrar*: to unbalance. That was the role I saw for Kewell, coming on to unbalance Milan.

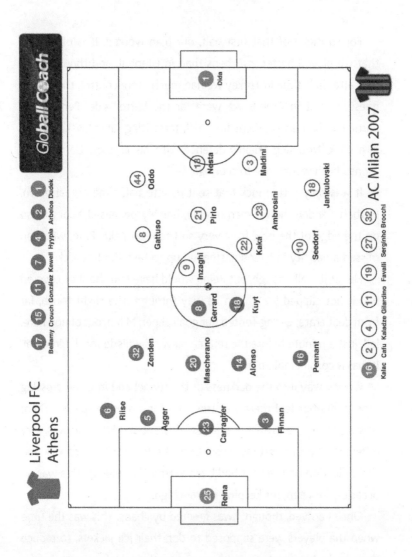

Milan, two years on, were even more reliant on the runs of Kaka than they had been in 2005, and we deployed both Mascherano and Alonso to keep track of him. Our idea was to make the most of the space left by Oddo and Jankulovski, with Gerrard playing as a second striker off Kuyt, trying to win second balls.

For so much of that first half, our plan worked. It is often said that we played better in Athens than in Istanbul, and though I feel that after half-time in Turkey we had much more control, there is no question that in Athens we were far the better side. Pennant, in particular, had an excellent first half, terrorising Jankulovski, forcing him back, troubling Milan's defence with his crosses. Gerrard and Alonso both went close to scoring.

It was only rotten luck that sent us into half-time a goal down. Herbert Fandel, the German referee, harshly penalised Xabi Alonso on the edge of the box, for a very soft foul on Kaka. Pirlo, who had missed a penalty in Istanbul, stepped up to take the free kick.

He hit it well enough, but Reina would have had the shot covered had it not clipped Inzaghi on its way through. The slight touch, far from deliberate, wrong-footed our goalkeeper. Milan, out of nowhere, led, just a minute before the referee blew his whistle for the interval. It was a considerable blow.

On my way into the darkness of the tunnel and into the dressing room, I did not feel there was the need for a rousing speech. There was no reason to invoke memories of Istanbul. My mood was very different. The circumstances too. Both the foul for the free kick and the deflection on the shot had been extremely unlucky. This was an occasion for calm, for keeping morale high.

Once I arrived, though, I was greeted by chaos. This was the time when the players were supposed to don their ice jackets, to reduce their body temperatures and maximise their performance in the second half. Everyone was running round, making sure the jackets were working, that every player had one for two or three minutes.

'Sit down,' I said, when I had taken in the scene. 'We cannot worry about all of these things. We have to deal with the most important thing: the football match.' It was hardly ideal to get a message across when everyone was rushing around. I needed their attention.

'Carry on doing the same things,' I told the players, as things settled. 'There is space behind the defence. We have been really unlucky. We don't deserve to be losing. We are doing the right things, making chances. Stay on top of them.'

The plan was fine. Our strategy was working; we were doing well. There was no reason to change things. As I had always intended, fifteen minutes into the second half, I put Kewell on for Zenden. Almost immediately, Gattuso played a poor pass and Gerrard might have scored, but Dida saved his shot.

We poured forward, but Milan, to their credit, stood firm. We sustained our attacks, won every second ball, ratcheted up the pressure. We could not find a way through.

Perhaps that was the difference from Istanbul. In 2005, Ancelotti's team were so convinced of their superiority that they continued to attack even when they were leading by three goals. Two years on, they were more cautious. They knew what we could do to them if they gave us even the slightest opportunity.

A manager finds himself in a quandary at such moments. You are the better team, going forward, controlling the game. And yet the clock is ticking. Time is running out. We had only fifteen or twenty minutes to find a goal or we would lose the European Cup final, the biggest game in club football. It is easy to say that the solution is to send a striker on. But when your team is doing well, when there are no obvious weak points, changing the system can sometimes make things worse.

Fourteen minutes. Thirteen. Twelve. I sent on Crouch, for Mascherano. Gerrard dropped into midfield. We had to gamble, and hope it came up red.

It did not pay off. The ball landed on red-and-black. Milan, breaking up one of our attacks, worked the ball clear to Kaka, roaming in the area where Mascherano would have picked him up. The Brazilian, enjoying a rare glimpse of time and space, slipped the ball to Inzaghi, who raced clear. He rounded Pepe Reina. Our goalkeeper was on his knees. Inzaghi tucked the ball into the net. There were eight minutes left.

We did all we could. I sent on Alvaro Arbeloa so that we could play with two defenders and, effectively, eight attackers. That may seem a strange substitution at 2–0 down in a European Cup final with two minutes to play, but we needed to win the ball back if we were to keep going forward.

We pulled one back, a header from Kuyt.

For just a second, everything stopped. This would be a comeback even more remarkable than Istanbul. We had just moments to find another goal. To take it into extra time. Into injury time.

And then, it was over. All that work, all that effort. Over. We were beaten.

I marched onto the pitch, my players on their backs, distraught, all around me, their opponents celebrating as wildly as we had two years previously. Fandel, the referee, was the target of my ire. He had played just two minutes and forty-five seconds of injury time, when there were supposed to be three, plus another thirty seconds for a late substitution made by Ancelotti.

'We had just scored once and you blew the whistle in the middle of an attack,' I shouted, above the roar of Milan's fans. 'You blew early.' He would not even look me in the eye. He stalked off, to the sanctuary of the dressing room.

There is nothing that can be said to players at those moments. Losing a normal game is hard enough, but a final? It is difficult to describe the anguish of standing on the pitch, applauding your opponents as they collect their medals, as they lift the trophy, as they embrace each other in delight. All that you might have had, they have taken. It is a pain so sharp as to be exquisite. Each player needs their own time to come to terms with what has happened, their own space to mourn.

I do not know how long we stayed on the pitch, everyone alone with their thoughts. I shook hands with Ancelotti, a good man, and Ariedo Braida, the club's influential director, as they celebrated. They took time to express their respect for what we had achieved. Silvio Berlusconi, later that evening, would seek me out too, and offer his condolences and congratulations. All three came across as gentlemen.

When we returned to the dressing room, I tried to console each one of my players, to find a kind word for everyone, though you cannot say too much. No matter how hard they have tried, no matter how much they did, they know they have lost. It was not enough. It is only later, when everything has sunk in, that you can try to talk things through.

* * *

We did not have a party that night. It was more of a wake. We returned to our dark, uncomfortable hotel, deep in Athens' sprawling suburbs, to have a meal and a drink with the coaching staff and their families, to commiserate with each other, to discuss what went wrong.

It was 1 a.m., perhaps later, when we arrived back from the stadium, and it was not until 3 a.m. that we were ready to go to sleep. There was a problem, though: several of our wives, who had joined us for the meal, had nowhere to sleep. I agreed to allow Montse and Noemi, the wife of our chief scout Eduardo Maciá, to share our room.

Her husband and I would have to stay up.

It was a wet, miserable night, but I think we both needed to get out of that claustrophobic hotel. At 3 a.m., we put on our black overcoats and went for a walk in the teeming rain, in an unfamiliar city.

We strolled round Athens for four hours. We discussed everything. We analysed the game, what we might have done differently, where we could have improved. We went over every decision in the game, tactically and technically, and examined the referee's performance too.

Then, when we had exhausted that, we discussed the future, the players we were considering signing, how we hoped to develop the academy, what we needed to do to make sure we could reach another European Cup final, and win it. We talked about staff, how to organise the club, about our vision, our project.

It was past 7 a.m. when we returned to the hotel, soaking wet. In just two or three hours I would have to give a press conference. I knew exactly what I was going to say. There was a message that needed to be broadcast. A warning that needed to be heeded.

'The owners tell me they want to win the Premiership and the Champions League,' I told the assembled media a few hours later. The mood in the hotel was forlorn. I had passed Steven Gerrard sitting on the stairs, disconsolate, on my way down to the room which had been adapted to accommodate the world's press.

'They can, but they need to understand the business here. We need to do things quicker than Chelsea and Manchester United. If we don't spend money, change things, improve in a lot of areas, we could fight to finish fourth. The owners understand and support me, and say they will back me. But if we don't change things, we will not be contenders.'

That press conference was interpreted as an attack on Hicks and Gillett, on the club. But I was not too concerned with how the media portrayed it. I simply wanted the club to progress. We did not have as much money as United or Chelsea, that was clear. If you don't have the money, then you have to work faster, better, in the market than anyone else. It was not an attempt to attack anyone; I simply wanted to help the club, my club, end its wait for a Premier League title, as well as retain its status as one of the most feared teams in Europe.

'We have the names to improve the squad, but we need to do it,' I continued. 'This is a crucial time. The conversations with the new owners are really good. They say I can do this and this and this. OK.

I am trying, but when? I start to do something, and then we cannot finish. It is something to do with the structure of the club, and we must change it. If we don't, we will lose targets.

'Have Carra and Stevie signed contracts? I am asking you. What about Xabi or Reina? I was with Xabi and others after the game. We talked about the opposition, the tactics we had. It is normal. Players like Xabi, Reina, Gerrard, Carra, they want to know you have good players ready to sign. We were talking about the fact that renewing the contracts of key players would send a message to others that we want to build a strong team. But if we waste time, we can't sign the players we want.'

My message was a simple one. The owners had to realise that everything depended on doing things quicker. We had to be more decisive. I wanted them to see that we had been to a second Champions League final in three years and it was now time to strike out for the next level.

And their reaction, at that time, was good. They had flown straight back across the Atlantic after watching the game in Athens, but we spoke soon after the game and they were really pleased. They were happy with what I had said, with my desire to see things improve in all aspects of the club. They knew it had not been an attack, but a warning. They knew everything was moving too slowly. They agreed with me. That was how they wanted to do things too, they said.

We would see.

4

Season 2007–08
Force of Nature

ON THE COFFEE TABLE IN FRONT OF ME LAY A SINGLE SHEET of paper. Written on it were a dozen or so names.

It was a few weeks before we were due to face AC Milan in the 2007 Champions League final in Athens. I had gathered some of my most trusted staff together in my office. We had a decision to make.

That piece of paper was the product of months of intense scouting. A manager will start planning the new season as much as six months before the end of the current campaign. Your squad must be analysed, your weaknesses assessed, your possibilities in the market examined.

We knew, despite the presence of Dirk Kuyt and Peter Crouch, that if we were to progress as a club, we needed to make at least one headline signing, to capture a player that would make the rest of Europe sit up and take notice, and that it would have to be a striker.

We had dispatched scouts across the world to identify candidates, and we had narrowed all of those players down to a dozen or so, all famous names, all attainable, all boasting different abilities, all with varying strengths and weaknesses.

Over the course of the next three or four hours, we would whittle that list down from a dozen to one; the one man who we could task with restoring Liverpool to the pinnacle of English and European football.

One by one, we discussed each candidate.

Julio Cruz, of Internazionale. A hugely experienced, technically adept Argentine, available relatively cheaply. His ability in the air would suit the English game.

Amauri, a Brazilian playing at Palermo, in Italy. He had risen from nowhere to become one of the most feared strikers in Serie A, first with Chievo Verona, then with the Sicilian team, though an injury had curtailed his season prematurely.

Lisandro López, another Argentine, of Porto. He was mobile, strong, with an excellent shot.

Alberto Gilardino, of AC Milan. We would encounter him a few weeks later in the Greek capital, of course, a late substitute for Pippo Inzaghi, after his team-mate had done so much to destroy our dreams. He had pace. He held the ball up well.

Perhaps eight more had their relative merits discussed, their cost, their wages, how they would adapt to life in England, how they would fit into our team. We dissected some of the biggest names in European football in the course of an afternoon, until we had chosen our one.

A few days later, I called him. Initially, he did not answer. But late on a Sunday evening, when I was out walking the dogs by the beach, I saw that he had called back. I rang him straightaway.

'*Sí*,' he said, when he picked up.

'*Hola*, Fernando,' I replied. 'Do you know who this is?'

'No. I've had three calls from this number. Who is it?'

'It's Rafa Benítez.'

Fernando Torres, though, was suspicious. He thought it was a prank, similar to the one which had caught out José Antonio Reyes a few months previously. Reyes, while with Arsenal, had been tricked by a Spanish radio station into thinking he was talking to Emilio Butragueño, the Real Madrid director, and poured his heart out about his desire to leave London and move to the Bernabéu. Torres did not want to fall victim to the same routine.

I did all I could to persuade him. I explained to him how I saw him fitting into our side, what I thought we could achieve with him at Anfield, talked a little about life in England and playing in the Premier League. I needed to know if he was interested, if he was worth pursuing. He was shy, softly spoken, but he knew how good an opportunity this was. He did not want to waste it. He encouraged me to speak with Miguel Angel Gil, Atlético's chief executive, to strike a deal. He would become, at the time, the most expensive signing in Liverpool's history. But we knew we had found the player we wanted, we needed. He had pace, he was good in the air and, most of all, he had tremendous hunger, to improve himself, to win trophies. He was the right age, and he was within our budget. He fitted the bill exactly.

We fitted him too. He would be distraught to leave Atlético, after twelve years at the club he had supported throughout his life, but I did all I could to convince him that what we were building was tremendously special.

That summer, the Americans seemed to have heeded what I said in the aftermath of Athens. We wanted to move forward, to become the most successful team in Europe. We moved quicker. Things weren't perfect, but they were definitely better.

The Americans accepted, at that stage, that their knowledge of football was limited. They were using Gillett's son, Foster, as an advisor almost, because he had researched players on the internet and he could interpret statistics. They were pleased with our idea of signing some senior players, some younger players and some foreign players for the academy, in order to meet UEFA's looming home-grown guidelines in the future. I spoke to Hicks about our vision at length. His concern was more with signing players for the first-team than the future, but at least we were being given the opportunity to strengthen our squad.

I knew that we would have to complete the deal for Torres as soon as possible, so I flew out to Madrid at the first available opportunity, alongside Rick Parry, to open formal negotiations with Atlético. They progressed reasonably well, but for a while it looked like we would not manage to finalise terms. Rick was to fly back that night, but I convinced him to delay the flight for as long as we needed. 'If we don't do it now, we might lose him for good,' I said.

By the time we returned to Liverpool late that night, we had the basis of a transfer in place. We would need to get everything signed and sealed as soon as possible, though. I did not want another club to get wind of our interest and try to outbid us. I arranged for Fernando, his agents and his girlfriend, Olalla, to fly to England. We would continue conversations there.

The party was picked up the next night at John Lennon Airport and whisked to a beautiful waterfront apartment in the city, complete with underground parking. Nobody was to know Fernando was in Liverpool. We could not afford for the news to leak out. Only four or five people at the club knew how advanced the deal was, plus a handful of his close associates and the directors at Atlético.

The weather – for that week, at least – was glorious. Liverpool is a particularly wonderful city in the sunshine. From their luxury flat, Fernando and Olalla had a great view across the Mersey and of the city's skyline.

They would have plenty of time to enjoy it. For two days, they were not permitted to leave the apartment. Their agents would leave, to join us for contractual discussions, and progress was relayed to Fernando on the telephone. He had plenty of work to do, though: as well as providing him with food from restaurants in the city, we sent him countless books and DVDs of Liverpool's greatest players and finest moments, descriptions of the club's history, images of its achievements. For forty-eight hours, we deluged him with Liverpool's folklore. And all the time, I spoke with him by phone, telling him how I wanted the team to play, what I wanted him to do, how he could help us win trophies and titles.

Eventually, the deal was done. Fernando was a Liverpool player.

'The Liverpool offer arrived and I told the club to listen to only that one,' he said, after posing for photos in his new number nine shirt at Melwood and Anfield. 'This is the team I wanted to play for. It is one of the best, if not the best, in Europe. The fact that Liverpool are giving me the number nine shirt just goes to show the confidence they have placed in me. This is a unique opportunity. Liverpool aspire to everything, and that has been an important factor in my decision.'

He had been convinced: all of those DVDs, all of those books, all of those clandestine phone calls to that penthouse flat had not been wasted. Fernando could see what we wanted to do.

As well as Torres, we signed Yossi Benayoun and Ryan Babel, two players who could help us be more effective going forward. Their arrivals were not a slight on the side we had already; we just knew we needed to go to the next level.

There is a human element to strengthening your side, a huge number of consequences for every decision you make. Peter Crouch, for instance, would eventually find his opportunities so restricted by Torres that he felt the need to force a move to Portsmouth. He had found life at Liverpool difficult initially, of course, as he endured that long goalless streak, but he had become a valued member of the team, and he was a hugely well-liked member of the squad. A club, though, always has to move on.

* * *

The relationship between the manager and the fans is what sets Liverpool apart from other clubs. It is different. It is special.

Liverpool is, comparatively, a small city. Everyone knows what everyone else is doing. That makes it a tight-knit local community, with a real sense of empathy and unity between all the people who live there. It is the same with the club.

From the very first day I arrived, the fans had offered me a warm welcome. They had always been incredibly supportive. They were quick to let me know that, even when times were tough, they appreciated that I was working hard for the club, and for them, that I was doing my best. It is not always like that elsewhere. There is a real bond between the manager and the people who come, every other week, to watch the team.

But, as our bus slowed down to approach Anfield just a couple of hours before we were due to play FC Porto in a game that would decide not only our fate in that year's Champions League but, possibly, my future at the club, I could not believe what I was seeing. I had never seen fans like this before, so dedicated, so loyal to a foreigner. It was a moment that touched me deeply.

We had qualified for the Champions League that year with relative ease. A single goal from Andriy Voronin had given us a 1–0 win on a baking-hot day against Toulouse in the first leg of our qualifier in France. The return fixture had been rather more straightforward: we had taken the lead in the first half through Peter Crouch, doubled our advantage immediately after half-time thanks to Sami Hyypia, and Dirk Kuyt had scored twice in the last few minutes to see us through 5–0 on aggregate.

The group draw had pitted us against Porto, the Portuguese champions, Marseille, of France, and the Turkish team Besiktas. We knew it would not be easy, but just a few months after we had come within a whisker of winning the competition, we were clear favourites to reach the knockout stages for the fourth season in succession.

We played what looked like our hardest game in the group first, a trip to northern Portugal and the imposing, atmospheric Estadio do Dragao. That was a fine Porto team, full of internationals: José Bosingwa, Bruno Alves and the Uruguayan Jorge Fucile in defence; Raúl Meireles in midfield, with the Argentine Lucho González and his countryman Lisandro López, whom we had considered signing, in attack. Ricardo Quaresma, a quicksilver winger, was their main creative outlet.

The first ten minutes of the game proved how daunting our task that night was. Our hosts swarmed forward straightaway, and we might have been behind almost immediately, but for Pepe Reina saving from López. We would not be so lucky a few minutes later, our goalkeeper bringing down Tarik Sektioui in the penalty area. Reina could not save González's spot-kick.

It was the worst possible start, but we recovered quickly. Kuyt equalised, with a header, less than ten minutes later.

Porto were still dangerous, though, and any hope we had of taking control of the game disappeared when Jermaine Pennant was sent off early in the second half, for a second yellow card. We had half an hour to hang on, playing in a 4–4–1 formation, simply trying to see the game out. Given the circumstances, we were happy to emerge with a 1–1 draw, after Porto's immensely strong start and the dismissal of Pennant.

However, our form in the Premier League, where we were unbeaten, was good, and we felt confident we would be able to improve in our next two Champions League games, against Marseille at Anfield and Besiktas in Turkey. It would not play out that way.

Marseille's visit to Merseyside was especially disappointing. Eric Gerets, their manager, had only just taken charge of the French team and their league form was very poor. At Anfield, though, they were well organised in defence, dedicated in midfield and worked extremely hard. I remember both Sebastian Leto, an Argentine winger, and Mohamed Sissoko being criticised for their performances in that game, but in truth, the entire team struggled to take control of the match. Even with Anfield behind us, even with all of our European experience, we just could not break Marseille down.

And then, as time ran out, the visitors scored. It was a brilliant goal too, from Mathieu Valbuena, their diminutive playmaker, who sent a shot dipping and curling over Reina. We did not have the time or the opportunities to find an equaliser. It was the first time we had lost a group-stage game at Anfield in four years.

That defeat left us in a very difficult position, with just a point from our first two games. Suddenly, our trip to Istanbul, a scene of such happy memories, acquired considerably more significance. In those circumstances, there is no worse place to go.

The noise at Inonu, Besiktas's stadium, is incessant, intimidating. For three hours before the game, they are singing their songs, banging their drums, lighting their flares; during the match, they do not stop, not for a second. Anfield is impressive on European nights, but Inonu is a wall of sound.

It is hard to say how much an atmosphere can affect players, but it is certainly one aspect that a club can control in an attempt to gain an advantage. That trip to Istanbul convinced me that we needed to do more to harness Anfield's power. When I first arrived at Liverpool, we played our anthem, 'You'll Never Walk Alone', when the players were in the tunnel. When it was finished, after the rousing end to the song, the teams would walk out onto the pitch. That cost us momentum.

I petitioned the club to change things round, so that the players came out to the sound of the fans singing, but was told that the rules in both the Premier League and the Champions League made it impossible. I persisted and, eventually, we decided to do it. It was criticised, but it is a crucial factor. Hearing Anfield in full voice inspired our players and, just maybe, intimidated our opponents.

Admittedly, a more important factor in Istanbul than the un-ceasing roar of Besiktas's crowd was the poor quality of the pitch, which meant that we could not move the ball properly. From the start, sensing our discomfort, our Turkish hosts hurled themselves forward. We were sluggish, nervous, unable to take control. Just as we had in Portugal, we conceded early, a shot deflecting off Hyypia's leg and past Reina. The noise increased. The drums beat faster. The sound washed down the stands and seemed to double Besiktas's resolve.

We pressed and pressed for an equaliser. Voronin missed the ball from three yards out. The goalkeeper kept out a shot from Gerrard. Hyypia, too, almost scored.

With eight minutes to play, we were punished. Bobo, a tricky Brazilian winger, slipped the ball under Reina on the counter-attack. Gerrard pulled one back almost immediately, but we ran out of time. One point from three matches. We were on the brink of elimination from the Champions League at the group stage. Our proud record, our reputation as a genuine European force, was under threat.

Off the pitch, too, problems were mounting. The Americans had kept their promises in the transfer market that summer, helping us to bring in players, but our relationship was starting to grow strained.

In early November, I had been trying to communicate to them the need to start planning for the January transfer window, to begin considering our options for strengthening our side. I did not want a specific amount of money – I never asked them to put a definitive figure on how much they would make available – but I wanted us to move as quickly as we could to make sure that we did not miss out. They were evasive. They would not give me the go-ahead to start talking to players and agents to see if they wanted to join us. I was communicating with the owners mainly by email, and it was hard to get a clear response from them about what we would be able to do.

I heard a host of rumours and whispers from people in the game. Hicks and Gillett, they told me, had met with Jurgen Klinsmann, the former German national team manager, to see if he would be interested in managing Liverpool. My friends, people I trust, whose information is usually correct, told me my own employers were planning to replace me. Whenever I challenged anyone about it, they denied it, but I knew it was true.

Even with my position uncertain, I tried to keep working.

We were still unbeaten in the league, but we knew that we had no room for mistakes in the Champions League, starting with the visit of Besiktas at home. That game would prove to be a turning point. A statement of intent.

The 8–0 scoreline remains a record for the Champions League to this day. No other team has won by that margin in the modern tournament's history. We led by two at half-time, thanks to Crouch and Benayoun, but in the second half, we sent out a message, to our supporters, our owners and the rest of Europe. Liverpool were not quite finished yet.

In those forty-five minutes, we scored six times. Crouch got one, Benayoun another two – completing his hat-trick – Gerrard scored once and Ryan Babel, a substitute, added another two in the twenty-seven minutes he was on the pitch. It was a special game, proof that we were a force to be reckoned with.

It is easy for teams, when they are leading by two or three goals, simply to switch off, to cruise through until the end of the game, conserving their energy, playing out time. My experience in Madrid means that I have a very different approach. I always want my players to score more. I do not believe in relaxing, not until the game is at an end. A team should always play at its most intense. That was what we did that night, and we were rewarded. Perhaps someone will beat that record, scoring more than eight goals, but that it is yet to happen is a source of great pride.

Still, I tried to keep planning. In the week leading up to our Premier League game with Newcastle, I was emailing the owners about a player I wanted to sign in January. They were still relatively inexperienced when it came to doing deals, and I thought I could save them some money. Hicks's response, written in capital letters, was brusque and to the point: I was to focus on coaching and training the team I already had. Discussion over.

I was furious. The owners simply did not understand how we had to work if we wanted to catch Manchester United and Chelsea without matching their funds; they would not even listen when I was trying to save them, and the club, some money.

The previous season, we had managed a club-record eighty-two points in the Premier League. There was huge expectation that this would be the year we would be able to take on the richest clubs in the division. There was huge pressure on all of us – manager, staff and players.

Not only would they not listen to my argument that we needed to try to strengthen the side in January so that we might be able to fulfil our supporters' hopes, they were actively considering replacing me. I felt hurt and betrayed, but all I could do was keep on working. All I could do, in fact, was concentrate on coaching and training my team, the players I already had.

It all came to a head, of course, in that famous press conference at Melwood, when I repeated the phrase Hicks had sent to me in answer to a succession of questions from confused reporters. It was not something our media team were expecting, but my intention was always the same: to do the best thing for the club.

That weekend, as I unpacked in our team hotel in Newcastle, I realised I had forgotten to pack a pair of shoes to wear with my suit.

I only had trainers with me. It is not something I ordinarily do, but I would have to wear a tracksuit on the touchline. It was seen as a continuation of my protest – that I was merely a coach, nothing more – but, in fact, it was testament to nothing other than my own forgetfulness.

That a simple error made when packing a bag could be read in such a way by our fans showed how strained things were at the club at that time. The following day – after a slew of stories in the weekend's newspapers that both José Mourinho and Klinsmann were being lined up to replace me if we failed to beat Porto and were eliminated from the Champions League – the owners released a statement on our website saying only that they had nothing to add in response. Normally, a club would be at pains to dismiss such rumours as just gossip. Not this time.

Suddenly, the fans could see it was not simply media speculation. Defeat to Porto could cost me my job. And, because of that special bond, that unique relationship, our supporters started to plan.

I had been told there would be a march in my honour before Porto's visit. Friends had seen posts on a variety of messageboards on the internet suggesting the idea, while others had been told what a group of fans were thinking about doing. I had never heard of such a thing happening for a manager, let alone a foreigner, born thousands of miles away. That is Liverpool, though. That is why it is special.

We did not see the march, of course, from the dressing room, but we had seen the fans, as many as 2,000, gathering before the game and heard the cheer when the bus appeared at the Paisley Gates, by the Hillsborough memorial. We had seen the Spanish flags flying and the banners. One, which I was shown later, read: 'You're the custodians, it's our club. Rafa stays.' That is a sentiment which meant everything to me.

I did not, though, see the Rafatollah, the gilt-edged picture of me from my time in Valencia which was carried aloft at the front of the crowd as it made its way down Anfield Road. But it did not matter. I knew what the fans had done for me. I knew that I had to do all I could, to work even harder, to make sure that I deserved their support.

The most important thing, though, was not to let the problems with the owners, the disputes and the doubts over my future distract the players from the task in hand. We had to win the game, of course, and we knew too that we had to give the sort of performance the fans deserved, one that showed how much we appreciated their support.

We managed to do so. As soon as the anthem died down, I heard my name sung by the Kop. The rest of the stadium soon picked up the tune. It is the loudest I have ever heard my name chanted, anywhere, in my entire career. It was a special moment, from special fans.

We took the lead through Torres, his first goal for us in the Champions League, a header from a Gerrard corner. Porto equalised, through López again, another header. We pushed and pushed for another, pressing Porto back, harrying them out of possession, trying to get the ball into wide areas, but it was not until the last few minutes that we earned our reward, the goal that kept our hopes of reaching the knockout stages alive.

Torres picked up the ball on the left-hand side of the penalty area and bent it round Helton, Porto's goalkeeper. Anfield breathed a sigh of relief. At that stage, I was thinking only about the game, trying to pass messages to players to make sure we did not allow our opponents back into the match, but looking back, that was a hugely important goal for my career at Liverpool. We were in control of the game, and I was in control once more.

We would add two more – a Gerrard penalty and a header from Crouch – to make sure we gave the fans exactly what they wanted, a resounding 4–1 win and the knowledge that if we won our final group game, at Marseille, we would be in the last sixteen of the competition once again. It was the least they deserved, for all the support they had given me.

'I want to say thank you to our supporters, because I think they were, as always, magnificent,' I said, as soon as I had sat down behind the raised desk in the trophy room to give my post-match press conference. Their faith and loyalty had made me extremely happy. I wanted to show them how grateful I was, how much what I had seen meant to me.

'The most important thing is the team, so I say thank you for the support. To the players, it was important, as I said before the game, and it was important for me, so I say a thank you, a big thank you.'

It was also a chance for me to try to repair relationships with the owners. All I had wanted to do was to make sure we were thinking about the future, that we were doing all we could to make the club as good as it could be. Conflict between the boardroom and the boot room could only serve to hurt Liverpool.

'My relationship with them was good before, and now we need to talk about what the problem was,' I said, when one of the journalists, seated either side of a bank of television cameras, asked about the issues of the previous few weeks. 'I don't have any personal problems with them. I am sure we will talk and they will understand and I will understand their ideas. It is not my ego, it's my responsibility. I need to take care of my team, my squad and this club.'

It was several weeks later that we did, finally, meet face to face. In the Anfield boardroom, after a game against Manchester United in the Premier League, I asked them if they had approached Jurgen Klinsmann about my job. They admitted they had met him, but said that it was only to discuss issues about marketing, that sort of thing. It was an unconvincing explanation. Only two or three months later did they reveal the truth, or a version of it: that they had met Klinsmann in case I decided to leave Liverpool for Real Madrid.

It was obvious, by that stage, that all was not as it seemed with the owners. There had been no 'spade in the ground' on the new stadium they had promised to build, and there were suggestions that they were placing debt on the club, meaning the money we would have used to strengthen the squad would now go to repay interest. It was starting to seem that there were now other priorities at Liverpool, rather than just what was happening on the pitch.

By the time I met Hicks and Gillett, we had at least guaranteed our place in the last sixteen of the Champions League. After Porto, we had just one game to go, one final hurdle to clear. Our performance at Marseille, two weeks after that show of support from the fans, stands out as one of the best of my time at Liverpool. We had complete control of the game, from the very first minute. We pressed relentlessly. We found space behind their full-backs, Taye Taiwo and Laurent Bonnart, who tended to go forward and leave their defence exposed. It was a professional, ruthless, impressive showing, at a time when we were under considerable pressure. We had to win, after all, and against a team that did not have any obvious weaknesses, as they had shown at Anfield.

When we were at our best, as we were in the Stade Velodrome that night, there were few teams who were capable of stopping us anywhere in Europe.

We had prepared for that game assiduously. As usual, I had worked twelve or fourteen hours every day in the build-up to our trip to Marseille, analysing our system and our opponents', trying to find an area we could exploit. And we had done all we could to keep the players relaxed, having gentle conversations and trying to laugh and joke, so that there was no risk of them seizing up under the pressure.

It worked.

Steven Gerrard scored as early as the fourth minute, winning a penalty and converting the rebound after his initial shot was saved. And then, a few minutes later, Torres scored one of the best goals I had the pleasure of seeing in my time at Liverpool, picking the ball up in that left-hand channel – where he had done so much damage against Porto – and wriggling clear of three or four defenders, twisting, turning, before beating Steve Mandanda. It was a wonderful strike. It was the sort of goal we had thought he would be able to score when we sat down, all those months before, and crossed out all of the names but his on that sheet of paper. With that goal, he proved how right we had been to identify him as the perfect signing for Liverpool.

Kuyt sealed victory in the second half, taking the score to 3–0, and Babel, on as a substitute, got a fourth on the counter-attack right at the very end of the game.

I was incredibly proud that night. It is an amazing feeling, winning when victory is absolutely essential, when the stakes are so high and the cost of failure so great. There are few more intimidating grounds in Europe than the Velodrome. We had shown no fear at all in sweeping past Marseille. We had managed sixteen goals in just three games. From the brink of elimination, we had qualified in style.

I have never worried about not sleeping. I will normally sleep for six or seven hours a night, waking up at six or seven in the morning, but if I wake earlier, I do not get anxious. I will simply go quietly downstairs to my office and get on with some work. It is the same after an evening game, when it is hard to go to sleep because of all the adrenaline in your body. I will take myself to my office, close the double doors and start preparing for the next game. There is always something to be done, whether it is noting down the things you remember about your last match, watching videos of the opposition, finalising reports; all of it needs taking care of and storing in the computer.

I have been using computers since my early days as a coach. I was always convinced, even when I was preparing my youth teams' training schedules on computers that ran on MS-DOS in the 1980s, that the computer would be able to help a manager store, access and interpret information. Training sessions and games produce a welter of data. It is useless, though, unless it is used properly. The program we use is a lot more sophisticated now, of course. It has been developed, steadily, throughout my career, from the early days of a ZX Spectrum and an Atari and the heart monitors and fitness belts I used at Real Madrid in 1990, to the state-of-the-art equipment we use today. The modern system has three separate functions. It analyses all of our games and all of our sessions; it helps construct training routines; and it can even design exercises with a specific target.

For example, say you want to improve how your team counter-attacks. The computer program will design a session with that in mind. It will select a number of possible exercises, each with the aim of making one aspect of your side's counter attack more fluid. It will change the exercises round, too, so that the players learn the same thing without getting bored. The target remains the same, but the exercise is different. That helps the squad enjoy themselves as they train.

After every training session and every match, we take all of the key information – our passes, our running, how we counter-attacked, how we defended, some feedback from players and staff – and we enter it, together with my notes, into the program. That then shows us what we need to improve on, the areas we must strengthen for the next game, what we should concentrate on in training. The program is adjusted all the time. Like a football team, it is constantly evolving.

The findings from the computer program are pored over by the analysis department, another incredibly valuable resource. They had their own room at Melwood, filled with monitors, where they would review our matches, watch footage of players we were considering signing and view scouting reports of our opponents. They would condense this information and, where necessary, prepare individual DVDs for the players.

The majority of our squad liked to analyse their own performances, to see where they were going wrong and where they were doing well. Gerrard, Carra, Fabio Aurelio, Martin Skrtel and Kuyt would often request videos. If you can show them their strengths and weaknesses, it helps them as players. Lucas Leiva, when we brought him over from Brazil, was particularly keen to learn. He would regularly sit in front of the screens with one of the coaches after training, to improve some aspect of his game. It is easier to show players things than simply tell them.

Others, like Fernando Torres, liked to see DVDs of their forthcoming opponents. In Torres's first season, in particular, when he was not so familiar with the Premier League's defenders, he would watch videos of the centre-backs he would encounter at the weekend. If he knew their movements, he would be able to adapt his game accordingly.

Sometimes, I would ask groups of players to go into the analysis room to watch a specific DVD. There was enough space, even in that cramped little room, for twelve players, as well as a member of the analysis department or one of my staff, if I could not make it. We would send the defenders in, say, or the midfielders, or perhaps the wingers with the full-backs. We would then try to explain to them what we wanted them to do and why. We would ask them what they thought about what they were watching, what was right and what was wrong. It has to be an interactive process. That way, the players know why you are asking them to do what you are asking them to do.

19 February 2008: Liverpool 2–0 Internazionale

Liverpool: Reina; Finnan, Carragher, Hyypia, Aurelio; Gerrard, Mascherano, Lucas (Crouch, 64), Babel (Pennant, 72); Kuyt, Torres
Internazionale: Julio Cesar; Maicon, Cordoba (Burdisso, 75), Materazzi, Chivu; Zanetti, Stankovic, Cambiasso, Maxwell; Cruz (Vieira, 55), Ibrahimovic

All of our analysis, all of our clips, all of the details emerging from the computer, all of the information we had pointed to one thing: if we were to beat Internazionale of Milan and take our place in the Champions League quarter-finals, we would need to isolate Marco Materazzi, Inter's tall, powerful, tattooed centre-back, and pit him against Fernando Torres, our fleet-footed, nimble striker.

The press conference room on the ground floor of Melwood, where we held our team talks, serves as a reminder of where Liverpool belongs, of what Liverpool is. There are quotes from Johan Cruyff and Diego Maradona on the walls, detailing their admiration for the

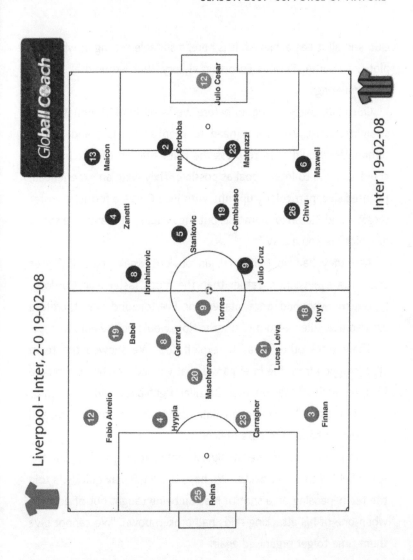

We knew Inter posed a threat, but we also knew we could hurt them: Mascherano would have to play close, very close, to our central defenders, because we could not afford to allow Cruz or Ibrahimovic any second balls; but to win, we knew Torres needed to isolate Marco Materazzi.

club and all it has achieved. It is here, a suitable setting in which to plot yet another famous European victory, that we hold all of our team meetings.

Our plan, thirty-six hours before we faced Inter at Anfield, was straightforward. We would need to keep a high line and a high tempo. We would have to press the ball as far up the pitch as we could, as close to Inter's goal as possible. They were an experienced, talented side, particularly upfront, with Julio Cruz – a former transfer target – and Zlatan Ibrahimovic, but they could not match the speed at which we could play.

And they had, in Materazzi, an obvious weak point. If Torres could run against him, rather than the much faster Ivan Cordoba, Materazzi, who had once played for Everton and was therefore assured a hostile welcome from the Kop, would not be able to cope.

There were other areas to exploit too. We showed the team clips, cropped from the Inter games that we had watched to prepare for the match, of Maicon, their Brazilian right-back, raiding forward.

'Fabio,' I said, 'don't overlap. Babel can beat him one-on-one, and you have to be alert in case Maicon starts to attack.'

That was the other Inter weakness that I felt we could exploit, the space behind their full-backs. 'We have to switch play quickly,' I told the team, pausing on a shot of Maicon being caught out of position when one of his attacking raids had broken down. 'We cannot give them time to get organised again.'

As always, we would have to be cautious at the back. Players of the quality of Cruz and Ibrahimovic would hold the ball up well, create space for Dejan Stankovic – playing between the lines –

and they were both excellent in the air. 'Javier,' I said to Mascherano, 'you must protect the central defenders. Stay in front of them, ready to win the second balls. Don't give Inter time and space to start playing.'

That was how we started the game. We switched play well, trying to isolate their full-backs, looking for space. And, as we expected, Materazzi struggled to cope against Torres, who could use his pace to beat him as we played the ball behind their defensive line. Twice inside the first thirty minutes, Materazzi was forced to foul our striker. Torres was just too quick for him. Materazzi simply could not keep up. Twice, he was shown a yellow card. Inter would now face an hour at Anfield with one player fewer.

Of course, that presents a very different challenge for the team with the extra man. It is often said that it is harder to play against ten men than against a side with all eleven, which is an exaggeration, but it certainly changes the tactical make-up of the match.

Roberto Mancini, the Inter manager, switched immediately to a 4–4–1 formation – which he would strengthen even further after half-time by introducing Patrick Vieira, the veteran defensive midfielder, to play wide on the right, to afford Maicon some protection. His priority now was to protect a clean sheet, and to strike on the counter-attack if it was at all possible.

Inter did all they could to slow the game down, defending deep, challenging us to pick our way through a blue-and-black wall, a line of players sitting not far from the edge of their own penalty area. They were narrow and compact, looking for set pieces to dull the tempo of the match and hoping to force our players, through frustration, into picking up yellow cards and, perhaps, evening out the numbers.

'Keep calm,' I told the team at half-time. 'We need to keep the tempo high. Don't give away possession. Make sure they have to keep running.' It is always much easier to play with the ball than without it. 'If we can get a two-on-one in the wide areas, go for it. Torres has to stay high, pushing them back, pushing. Don't take too many risks, don't be desperate. If we keep playing at the right tempo, switching play, we will get chances.'

Even with an extra player, though, there is a balance to be struck. Inter would look to pick us off on the counter-attack if they could, and we needed to guard against conceding the away goal. Javier Mascherano would have to redouble his efforts, patrolling the area in front of the central defenders to pick up second balls.

Midway through the second half, though, I was convinced that we were sufficiently well protected at the back to put on another striker. I replaced Lucas Leiva with Crouch, the idea being that we would be able to put more crosses in, to take advantage of the absence of Materazzi and the lack of height of Ivan Cordoba and Cristian Chivu.

Only very late on did we get our reward. Inter had defended extremely well, marshalled by Cordoba, but eventually our pressure on their full-backs told. Both goals came from attacking down our right wing, trying to isolate their left-back, Maxwell. First, Jermaine Pennant and Steve Finnan combined with Steven Gerrard to cross for Kuyt, whose shot bounced into the ground and over Julio Cesar.

Three minutes later, Pennant gave the ball to Gerrard, in the right-hand channel on the edge of Inter's penalty area, and his shot across Inter's Brazilian goalkeeper squeezed into the far corner of the Kop goal. He slid on his knees across the turf in celebration. We would now have a considerable advantage to take to San Siro.

Those goals changed the second leg of the tie immeasurably. Suddenly, we knew Inter would have to come forward; they would not be able to bide their time, be patient, and try to pick us off on the counter-attack. They would have to come out and play. The effect of that, of course, is that we would have much more space to counter-attack, the game would become more stretched, and we hoped we would be able to take advantage.

That is exactly how the game in Milan, two weeks later, played out. Inter were more attacking this time, playing in a 4–3–1–2 formation, at a higher tempo. They would pose a different problem from the one we had faced at Anfield.

It is easy at those times to try to defend deep, but that is something I have never liked to see in my teams, regardless of the circumstances or the quality of the opposition. The further back you are, the nearer you are to your own goal, the easier it is for the opposition to push you into a mistake. In San Siro, even as Inter swarmed forward, I wanted us to push out as much as we could, to keep switching play, particularly on their left, where I thought we might be able to find space, and through the middle, playing through Torres and using his speed. Steven Gerrard had said in our press conference the evening before the match that we had not travelled to Italy desperate only to defend; we wanted to attack Inter, to kill the tie, as quickly as we could.

To do that, of course, we needed to make sure they did not have a chance to reduce their deficit. Xabi Alonso had not been available for selection, as he decided to remain behind on Merseyside for the birth of his son, Jon, and so we started with Lucas and Mascherano as our central midfielders. We would keep a high line with our centre-backs and then keep that duo close, so that there was no space between the lines for Inter to play penetrating passes.

The Italian team started strongly. Julio Cruz, in particular, had one or two good opportunities to score, but could not find a way past Pepe Reina. Slowly but surely, we exerted more control over the game. Ryan Babel might have scored before the interval, but the decisive moment came just after the start of the second half. Nicolas Burdisso, playing in place of the suspended Materazzi, had already been booked when he bundled into Lucas on the half-way line. Tom Henning Ovrebo, the Norwegian referee, showed him a second yellow card. Yet again, Inter had not been able to keep all of their players on the pitch. That shows how difficult they found it to cope with the tempo at which we were capable of playing.

We did not have to wait long for the goal that all but assured us a place in the quarter-finals. Fabio Aurelio played a long pass to Torres, who controlled the ball and spun round Cristian Chivu in a single motion, before sending a shot past Julio Cesar.

That seemed to take all of the fight out of Inter. We were too well-organised to break down, and the knowledge that they needed to score four goals to progress was too much. The disintegration continued after the game was over, as the blue and yellow confetti that had accompanied our arrival on the pitch floated down from the stands, and the fans, who had started the match whistling our every touch, turned on their own players. That is how high the stakes are in these games: reputations, jobs, can be won and lost.

It seemed, by the end, that we had qualified relatively comfortably. It is only possible to give that impression when an enormous amount of hard work has been done beforehand, by the staff and the squad, to make sure the players know exactly what they have to do. It takes days of preparation, hours of videos and analysis and discussions, to get everyone ready for a game like that.

It can be a word, or a signal, or a shout, or a movement. It can come from one player, from two, or from half of the team. It can happen at any time, but it must happen at the right time, and only against certain teams.

'Press!'

Normally, it would be Xabi Alonso or Javier Mascherano, a central midfielder who has a broader vision of the play, who shouted to the team that we were to harry our opponents, close the ball down, try to regain possession, rather than waiting for them to make a mistake.

'Close!'

It is most effective if it is done in wide areas, for a very simple reason: if you press a player centrally, they can pass to their left or right, in front or behind. They have all four options potentially open. If you press them on the flank, one of those is closed off, and with a full-back facing them, they must normally come inside or play the ball backwards. This increases your chances of winning it back, or at least stifling their attack.

'Come on!'

It is not something any team can do throughout a match or all over the pitch, because it demands so much energy, so much commitment. And it is not especially effective when employed against a team who prefer to play long balls; then, it is much better to set up to try to win the second ball. Against a side who pass the ball well, though, pressing is crucial.

We practised pressing intensively in training, to make sure that on the signal – whatever that might be – the right players would react immediately and try to close the ball down, using a variety of exercises prepared by the staff.

If the ball was on our right, we would need the right full-back, the right winger and one of the central midfielders to press, and possibly a striker too. On the left, the opposite. It takes a long time to perfect the system, to make sure that players only do it when the moment is exactly right, when the ball is in an area you can press or the opposition have made a mistake, however slight. If you go too early, your rivals will be able to exploit the space that you leave behind, or take advantage of the brief disruption to your shape; too late, and the ball has already gone. Players have to be decisive, instinctive and determined to press; that is something that can be improved, and perfected, in training.

The importance of those routines, of those ceaseless drills designed to sharpen instinct, is made plain against a team like Arsenal, our opponents in the Champions League quarter-finals that season.

It was a team cast in Arsene Wenger's image, one which passed the ball beautifully, played at a quick, breathless tempo and boasted a host of players at their very peak: Emmanuel Adebayor, Robin van Persie, Cesc Fabregas, Kolo Toure, Emmanuel Eboue. If you give players of that calibre the space and time to find a rhythm, if you allow them to start weaving their passing patterns around you, then they can do untold damage. There is no choice but to press them, to try to regain the ball.

We would face Arsenal three times in six days in the first two weeks of April: twice in the Champions League, with the first leg at the Emirates Stadium and the second at Anfield, with a game in the Premier League, in north London, sandwiched in between.

Though they had stuttered a little in recent weeks, Arsenal were challenging for the Premier League title and, on paper, would probably have been many people's favourites to progress to the semi-finals. Our expertise that season lay in Europe, though, in the art of the knockout competition, the management of 180 minutes, the tactical preparation needed to overcome opponents expected to best us.

This was a competition no team understood better than us.

The first leg, in London, served to underline that. We set up in a 4–2–3–1 formation, with Ryan Babel on the left and Kuyt on the right, allowing Gerrard a lot of space between the lines, forcing one of Arsenal's midfielders, either Mathieu Flamini or Cesc Fabregas, to drop deep and cover him.

We pressed the ball well, using our pace to close our opponents down and regain the ball as high up the pitch as we could. Though we conceded first – failing to mark Adebayor from a corner routine – we equalised immediately. Gerrard, surging down the left, crossed low and Kuyt, a moment quicker in his mind than most players, beat Clichy to the ball and bundled home. We had not left England, but we had that crucial away goal.

Wenger did all he could to break free from our grip, introducing Theo Walcott – a young player we had tried to sign before he joined Arsenal – as a left-winger, to play against Jamie Carragher, filling in at right-back for us.

They had one or two chances – Martin Skrtel cleared one effort from the line, and Alexandar Hleb claimed a penalty for a foul by Dirk Kuyt – but we managed the game well. We stayed close to Arsenal's players, we were alert to their attempts to isolate our full-backs, their desire to overload on the wings, and we worked incredibly hard. We came away with the advantage. Wenger's team had won at San Siro, just as we had, in the previous round, beating AC Milan the week before we overcame Inter, but now they would have to travel to a far more imposing arena in desperate need of an away goal: Anfield.

8 April 2008: Liverpool 4–2 Arsenal

Liverpool: Reina; Carragher, Skrtel, Hyypia, Aurelio; Gerrard, Alonso, Mascherano, Kuyt (Arbeloa, 90); Torres (Riise, 87), Crouch (Babel, 78)
Arsenal: Almunia; K Toure, Gallas, Senderos, Clichy; Eboue (Walcott, 72), Flamini (Silva, 42), Fabregas, Diaby (Van Persie, 72), Hleb; Adebayor

Of all the qualities that convinced us, as we sat around discussing the names on that single sheet of paper in my office almost a year previously, that Fernando Torres was the right player for Liverpool, it was his hunger that stood out the most.

He had spent all of his career at Atlético Madrid, the team he had supported growing up in Fuenlabrada, a working-class district of the Spanish capital. Atlético, of course, have always existed in the shadow of Real, their larger, more successful neighbour, and even the presence of the player the Spanish called *El Niño* could not lift them above their rivals. Torres had matured into a full international and one of the finest strikers in Spain in his time at the Vicente Calderón, but he had not won a single trophy. He craved the chance to change that.

But he also had that crucial desire to improve himself as a player, to maximise his potential, to play in a team and alongside colleagues that allowed him to make the most of his talent. He did not yet know quite how good he could be. When he arrived, I promised we would make him even better. In doing so, we hoped we would be able to fulfil his desire to win trophies too.

Fernando was a willing pupil. As I have mentioned, we prepared DVDs for him, so he knew what to expect from the Premier League's defenders, who he had never encountered before, and the club helped him get up to speed with Liverpool's history, both as a team and as a city.

On the training ground, he was always trying to find ways to improve, to become more effective, more dangerous, and we never wasted an opportunity to help him adjust some small aspect of his game. There is a story that Fernando tells which describes how, after his first match since becoming a father for the first time, all of his team-mates were congratulating him in the dressing room on the birth of his daughter. I came in and congratulated him too. 'Well done,' I told him. 'You should be very proud. We've been working on your runs to the near post from corners, and it paid off for that goal.'

He looked confused and smiled. He hadn't told me he had become a father for the first time. I congratulated him on that too, of course, as soon as I found out!

The story shows, though, that we were doing all we could to help him: the goal he had scored that day had been the result of intensive work in training to help him make that run to the near post from corner kicks.

There was one other part of his game that we made sure to nurture all we could: his burgeoning relationship with Steven Gerrard.

Two players of such high quality will, usually, be on the same wavelength as each other, developing a special sort of bond, an instinctive ability to know what the other requires. Gerrard and Fernando were no different: it was clear, early on, that they would dovetail very nicely together. That must still be reinforced on the training pitch, though, by fine-tuning their play, helping them take up positions in which they can combine to the greatest extent, by working on patterns of play that will soon become ingrained in their memories.

Such exercises can involve three, four or five players, normally those who will be close together on the pitch. They are designed to teach those players specific movements, set actions that can be used during games. With Gerrard and Torres, we would go through maybe five or six routines to synchronise their runs; they would know where to go when the other was in a certain position. Their relationship was based on instinct, but those instincts can always be sharpened. Little by little, the relationship grows. Little by little, it becomes ever more devastating.

Fernando's impact was immediate. He scored in his first game at Anfield, racing down the left and curling a shot past Petr Cech in a 1–1 draw with Chelsea, and he produced several key goals – against Porto and Marseille in particular – that helped us through the Champions League group stage. He struck in San Siro, too, a beautiful, artful finish, to earn one of the most famous victories in Liverpool's illustrious history. His form in the Premier League was no less impressive: he would end the season having become the first Liverpool player for sixty years to score two successive hat-tricks at Anfield, and with a grand total of twenty-four goals, a record for a foreign player in his debut season.

It was on the night of the quarter-final second leg against Arsenal, though, that he scored the goal which encapsulated his first season at Liverpool. That was the night that, in my mind, he took his place among Anfield's greats.

It was a game played at breakneck speed in a feverish atmosphere, a match with the most thrilling conclusion imaginable.

Our idea was broadly the same as for the first leg. We would try to be narrow and compact in defence, pressing the ball intensely so that Arsenal could not get into a rhythm. Pepe Reina, we knew, would be particularly important as a sweeper, as Wenger's team would look to play a lot of penetrating passes along the ground. We would need to close down space well to interrupt their passing game.

We would start with a very attacking, very direct line-up: Torres alongside Peter Crouch – who had scored in the 1–1 draw the previous Saturday, when we met at the Emirates in the league – as strikers, with Gerrard wide right and Kuyt on the left. Mascherano and Alonso would have to manage space in midfield, trying to control the game and making sure we only pressed at the right time. We could not afford to allow Arsenal so much as a glimpse of an opportunity. We had the precious advantage of an away goal, but we knew that just one mistake would wipe that out.

Our plan was to play off Crouch, with Kuyt, Torres and Gerrard looking for the second balls. By playing so many attacking players, almost a 4–2–4, we hoped to be able to force Arsenal's defence back, creating space between the lines for our captain, in particular, to use.

For the first twenty-five minutes, we struggled to implement the plan. We could not close our opponents down, or break up their play. They scored an away goal, through Abou Diaby, after just thirteen minutes, and it was only after Sami Hyypia equalised – on the night and on aggregate – from a corner, that we began to assert a little bit of control. We were playing too direct, too quickly, and we were not winning second balls. Every time we cleared, the ball came back to us straightaway.

From a position of strength, we went in at half-time knowing we needed to improve vastly if we were to have any chance of reaching another semi-final. 'We have to keep pushing, pressing the ball,'

I told the players. 'But we have to be careful. They can counter-attack very quickly. We cannot let them catch us out.'

We improved after the break. We had more control, and Arsenal found it much more difficult to play through us. The tie was on a knife edge.

And that is when our plan that night, and our work with Fernando, paid off. Reina launched a long ball forward, towards Crouch. He was our outlet, allowing us to play long. The ball flicked to Torres, who controlled it, swivelled his body and curled a shot deep into the corner of the Kop goal. The whole stadium seemed to shake with visceral noise, infused with delight and relief. Fernando was buried under a pile of our jubilant players. We were almost there, in yet another semi-final.

Arsenal were not finished, though. Those last twenty minutes passed by in a blur. Wenger sent on Theo Walcott, yet again, on the right this time. To have such pace at your disposal so late in a game is always likely to be a huge advantage. It was his counter-attack, racing almost the length of the pitch, that set up Adebayor to slide home an equaliser. We had been caught out pushing forwards, as I had feared we would be. We would be eliminated on away goals unless we could score once more in the remaining six minutes or so. Anfield held its breath.

It is easy to talk about the twelfth man, about the impact your supporters can have on a game. Rarely have I seen it made flesh so clearly. From the kick-off, we poured forward. Ryan Babel, sent on as a substitute, cut inside and tried to ghost past Kolo Toure. The defender pulled him back. Penalty.

Steven Gerrard, needless to say, stepped up. The pressure must have been unimaginable. A player can have all the talent in the world, but if he does not have the right character, ability is irrelevant at such times. We had talked before the game about keeping calm, not letting the sense of occasion get to us, but it takes a special resolve to take on that awesome weight of responsibility.

That is what marks players like Gerrard out as something different. Even with an entire stadium, and millions of fans around the world, pushing him to score, he coolly converted the penalty. We led once more.

This time we would not be caught out. This time we kept our nerve, made sure Arsenal did not have space to play the passes that could hurt us. Tired legs chased them down when they were in possession, hurrying them, pressuring them. Mascherano and Alonso, in the middle of the pitch, controlled play, managed the game. In injury time, Babel burst forward, slicing through Arsenal's defence on the counter, his opponents melting away, and slotted home. This time, we knew we were there.

Our plan had worked at the very last, but it took an extra effort from the players to recover from Adebayor's goal. I made sure to highlight that when the celebrations had died down, when we had all left the pitch and I had walked to the trophy room to speak to the press.

'I was delighted with the belief, particularly in the second half,' I told the media. I wanted the players to know how proud I was of them, of the way they had reacted. 'When we went to 2–2 so near to the end, my players showed tremendous character and the desire to get up off the ground to win the tie. We were so poor before the break, but so much better in the second half.'

It was that character that had seen us through, that instinctive refusal to be beaten. It was something that all of our experience had given us, and that Anfield had nurtured too. Our stadium did not have the capacity of Camp Nou or the Bernabéu or San Siro, did not accommodate nearly so many fans, but there was no place in Europe that inspired quite the same fear that a trip to Stanley Park did. Our opponents in the semi-finals knew that only too well. Once again, it was Chelsea who barred our path to a third final in four years.

Little things can change everything. Seasons are decided and trophies lost on single moments, out of anybody's control. A cross is not blocked. A position is poor. A body shape wrong. And, suddenly, in a second, everything is different. History turns.

That year was the third in which Chelsea had travelled to Anfield for a Champions League semi-final, and it was the only occasion when they left feeling anything other than bitter disappointment and defeat. And yet it was the best we had played in any of our ties against them. It was still a well-balanced game, one of few chances and fine margins, but what chances there were fell to us.

The atmosphere, as always, was magnificent. The American owners were at the height of their battle for control of the club. Tom Hicks had decided to attend the game after we had met earlier in the week to discuss the future, but Gillett was absent, his place in the directors' box taken by representatives of DIC, who were attempting to buy his stake in the team. It was a war that was hugely destabilising, but that night it did not seem to matter: even as Hicks stood to sing 'You'll Never Walk Alone', there was no protest against him by the supporters. Everything was focused on beating Chelsea.

The team, certainly, had that one single aim in mind. Kuyt scored just before half-time to give us a deserved lead, and both Gerrard and Torres might have given us something of a cushion before the second leg, to put us in control of our destiny and, possibly, place one foot in the final, in Moscow. Only a succession of saves from Petr Cech, particularly in the last few minutes, kept us at bay, and allowed Avram Grant – who had replaced Mourinho earlier that season – a glimmer of hope.

But in a second, all that can be lost.

Five minutes into injury time, Salomon Kalou, a substitute, raced down Chelsea's left, attacking the Kop. Carra did not close him down quickly enough, and could not block his cross.

John Arne Riise, playing at left-back after replacing Fabio Aurelio, who was still not fully fit after his injury in Eindhoven, found himself caught out, too close to the goal, dealing with a ball he thought would not come into the box. His body shape was wrong. He knew he had to clear, as Nicolas Anelka was closing in, but misjudged his diving header. As he lay on the ground, the Kop goal rippled.

Disbelieving silence enveloped the ground. It was the last kick of the game, and suddenly Chelsea had the advantage.

There is little that you can say to a player in those circumstances. All I could do was try to support him as much as possible, to make him realise that nobody blamed him for the goal, that he had done his best and that such things can happen. John is a hugely dedicated player, who always gave his all for the club, and one who probably thought too much about what had happened, who churned over his mistakes in a game for days on end. He would not want to speak about what had happened for some time, but it was our responsibility to make sure he was not too hard on himself. That was all we could do.

There was no question that moment was the one that swung the tie, though. Travelling to Stamford Bridge leading by a goal rather than, effectively, losing by one would have made an enormous difference. We knew now that we needed to score if we were to make it to Moscow. Against a team desperate for revenge for the pain of 2005 and 2007, that would be especially difficult.

Chelsea might have changed manager, but they were as strong as ever. Planning the game, it was hard to pinpoint a player who could be pressed. They had played Paulo Ferreira at right-back at Anfield, but at Stamford Bridge they would draft in the powerful Michael Essien in that role, enabling them to build more from the back. The Ghanaian would carry the ball out of defence. At that time, he was one of the finest midfielders in the world. That is how strong their resources were, that he was not an automatic selection in his natural position. We knew we would have to be perfect to have any chance.

We did not start well in the rain in west London. Didier Drogba, a player we had identified as a threat before the game, put Chelsea ahead. When he scored the opening goal, he celebrated in front of our bench. To some, that could be a provocative act, but he was a player on the verge of a Champions League final. Of far greater concern to us was that Kalou – who had seen his shot saved by Reina before Drogba converted the rebound – seemed to be offside.

We recovered well. Yet again, we showed that we were not just a team of great ability and tactical intelligence, we had reserves of character too. Gerrard was much more influential in the second half, and when Yossi Benayoun played Torres through to equalise – on the night and in the tie – it was well deserved. Suddenly, Riise's mistake had been cancelled out. One more goal and we would be in Moscow.

It would not come. Neither side could find a way through in ninety minutes. Extra time beckoned. Yet again, there was little to separate us. Both teams were tired, and it is at those times that mistakes begin to creep into your play. A goal from Essien was ruled out for offside against four Chelsea players, despite their protests. A moment later, Sami Hyypia fouled Michael Ballack, and the hosts were awarded a penalty. Frank Lampard converted it. We needed a goal.

My reaction to that incident caused some consternation at the time. Immediately, I withdrew Torres, our leading scorer and talismanic striker, for Ryan Babel. Such a substitution may appear a strange decision, but it depends on the condition of the player. Some players do not struggle so much when their legs are tired, but others, like Torres, find it hard to make an impact when they have run out of energy. He needs to be fully fit to be at his best, and that evening, after a hundred minutes and with a slight hamstring injury, he was not. It was the best thing for the team to bring on a fresher player, despite the fact that Chelsea had just scored.

Babel would get his goal that night, of course, a long-range strike that fooled Cech, leaving him flat-footed, but by that stage Drogba had scored his second of the evening. We pushed all we could, but we could not find that third goal, the one that would have taken us to Moscow. It was over.

Stamford Bridge was exultant. Grant, my counterpart, sank to his knees in victory. For us, there was just desolation.

Of course I would have loved to be in another final, against Manchester United no less, but my first thoughts were for the players, the staff and the fans. What we had achieved that season was nevertheless remarkable – after all, Chelsea had spent a huge amount of money compared to us over the years – and I was still, as I told the media after the game, incredibly proud of everyone associated with the club. It was not good enough, though, when compared with the high standards we had set. We wanted to be in Moscow. We wanted the chance to regain our trophy.

However, I have a friend who puts all these things into perspective: remember, he tells me, that just as you and your players have people around you, wives and girlfriends, fathers and brothers, sons and daughters, who are disappointed when you lose, so do your opponents. If you had won, they would be just as crushed as you feel now. Someone has to lose. Someone has to be disappointed.

5

Season 2008–09
No More Worlds
Left to Conquer

BY THE TIME I ARRIVE AT MELWOOD AT AROUND 8.30 EVERY morning, I have already quickly scanned the morning's press in my office at home, enjoyed breakfast with my family and checked my emails, to make sure I am up to speed before my working day gets underway.

The first order of the day is always a meeting with my coaching staff. Arriving at roughly the same time as me, they meet with the doctor and the medical team before joining me in my office, so we know exactly which players are available to train, who can manage what workload and how various injuries are progressing.

That, in turn, influences our plans for training on any given day. Our season-long training schedule is broken up into micro-cycles of a week, or perhaps fifteen days, each one with a specific aim, depending on where we are in the season: early on, we might target training to build up stamina, while later in the campaign our emphasis might be on recuperation, or retaining possession, or a technical aspect of the game, such as refining our counter-attacks or honing our patterns of play. Sometimes we plan sessions that present the players with problems they have not encountered before, while at others we try to perfect things we have already worked on.

In that short meeting, we review what we want to do that day. If certain players are unavailable, we have to tweak our agenda, but, at all times, the aim remains the same: if we had intended to work on our patterns, for example, but Fernando Torres and Steven Gerrard are both injured, we might decide to do a possession routine instead.

At 9.30, those players who are currently injured arrive. They always have to be in earlier, so that we can make sure they are undergoing all the necessary treatments. A quarter of an hour later, the rest of the squad turn up, to have a quick chat with the medical team to update them on the progress of any niggling injury troubles, perhaps undergo a massage if necessary, and eat some breakfast. We have always found that players, if they eat breakfast at home, tend to have too much or too little; by offering food in the canteen, we are able to make sure they start the day exactly right.

Training begins at 10.30 and normally lasts for an hour and fifteen minutes, something like that. After the warm-up, the players not fit enough to join in the full session depart, to continue with physiotherapy or perhaps do some gym work, building up their fitness. The rest of us, meanwhile, get down to business.

A typical training session would be made up of four or five different exercises, each of them lasting around fifteen minutes. Take, for example, a morning designed to improve our finishing. We would start with a small-sided possession game, perhaps two against two, keeping the ball away from the players in the middle. Then we would move on to a shooting exercise in small goals, perhaps two players against one defender. Then perhaps a larger version, three on three maybe, before finishing off with a game of five-a-side. That could be one touch, two touches or 'all-in', if we are encouraging them to improve their dribbling skills.

Those games are not just a chance to have fun. Often, we set the teams involved scenarios: one side is a goal up with five minutes to go, say, or both sets of players can only score goals with one touch. If we finish the session with a game of ten against ten, on a full pitch, perhaps the situation can be more specific: it is the final of the Champions League, one team is leading by a goal to nil with ten minutes left. What do you do?

It is crucial that as many players as possible are involved at any one time. Most of our sessions are designed for sixteen, eighteen or twenty players, with each one taking a turn before standing aside for someone else, briefly catching their breath, and then going through the exercise again. It is not ideal to have lots of players standing and watching. It is best for them to be enjoying themselves, learning, practising and playing.

After a warm-down, we gather together the coaching staff and the medical team and analyse how the session has gone, check if any of us noticed an injury, or a player performing particularly well, or someone who did not seem to be quite at their best. We all make notes – to be fed into the computer later – and that, in turn, can alter what we do in the next day's session.

Once inside, I ask the doctor for a progress report on those players unable to train, before having a bite to eat, normally just a salad. At busy times in the season, I tend to eat at my desk, watching a game and scribbling some observations, or analysing information on the computer. There is no time to waste.

The afternoons can vary. Some players like to do extra fitness or technical work – added shooting practice, or an exercise to improve their touch, by playing a ball against a wall, for example – while others continue with their treatments. Even if they all go home, there is much work to be done.

If a group of players – the midfielders, or the defenders, or the full-backs and the wingers – are going to the video analysis suite to go through some footage, I will often go with them, along with Mauricio Pellegrino, my assistant, or some of the coaches, so that we can explain certain things on the DVDs they are watching, the aspects of play I want the players to concentrate on.

If not, it will be because I am embroiled in a meeting, with one of my scouts, or perhaps an agent, someone who has come to renegotiate a contract on behalf of a client, or because I am wading through reports of sessions, looking at information on the computer, preparing our forthcoming games.

And throughout it all, my phone rings incessantly. There is an occasional phone call from a journalist, though I try not to speak too much to the press: sometimes any information you choose to give them can be bad for the club, particularly in the transfer window, when it is crucial to keep your budget, your targets and such things as secret as possible.

But there are agents calling me, recommending players, asking who I am in the market to sign, or coaches who I know in England or Spain asking about players or simply discussing aspects of the game, how things are going. I like to talk to my scouts, too, based around the world, to find out who they are looking at and who they are excited about. Football, as so much, depends on information: the more you can glean, the better.

It would be impossible to get anything done if I was constantly talking to agents, though, so those I know to be reliable are passed on to the chief scout, and those I have not encountered before tend to be passed to my secretary. I do not have time for people who call up with long lists of players they are trying to allocate to clubs: I only want to deal with those who have someone special, someone who is right for Liverpool, that they want to recommend.

The day, often, does not end until seven in the evening. By that stage, I can scarcely wait to get home, to have dinner with my wife and my daughters and find out what they have done during the day, their news from school, and whatever has most recently captured their imaginations.

Sometimes, after dinner, we will go out for a walk along the beach close to our house with our dogs – Goofy, Honey, Red, a

German Shepherd, and our newest addition, Clem. That is my only downtime, I suppose, those evenings as a family, listening to the girls and talking to Montse about any number of subjects. We talk about football a little, though not so much. The girls have always been interested – Agata more so than Claudia – but, obviously, as a father, the most important thing is hearing what they are doing.

That summer of 2008 was one to drain the batteries on my mobile phone. There was much to do in the transfer market, and not very much time to do it in.

Several years previously, UEFA had introduced a new rule that stated that each club in the Champions League would have to name at least four 'home-grown' or British players in their squad for the competition in 2006, rising to six in 2007 and eight in 2008. The problems we had experienced with the academy failing to bring through young, local talent, though, meant that we had to come up with a plan to make sure we could comply with the laws. The club's under-eighteen team had won the FA Youth Cup in 2006, but with a host of foreign reserve players drafted in from our senior squad at Melwood.

Our strategy was this: according to UEFA's rules, a player could be counted as home-grown, wherever he was born, if he had been in a club's academy for three years by the time he turned twenty-one, which meant we could go and find talented youngsters abroad and bring them into our youth system. Over the course of three years, we would find ourselves with 'home-grown' players who were also of sufficient calibre to play in the first team.

That was the principle behind the signings of players like Emiliano Insúa, Daniel Pacheco, Daniel Ayala and Mikel San José; by the start of the 2009 season, all three would count as our own youth products.

At the same time, we would take control of the development of the most promising players already in the youth academy, to maximise their chances of emerging as first-team players. We designed a special programme to help Stephen Darby, a very slight young right-back, increase his strength. I told Jay Spearing, only 5' 6" but playing as a centre-back, that he would either have to be a defensive midfielder or a right-back. I encouraged Gary Ablett, who tragically died in 2012, to play Martin Kelly as a right-back, rather than a centre-back, to make best use of his pace and athleticism.

That was the best way to make sure that the 25-man squad list we submitted to UEFA in 2008 was as strong as possible; previously, we had been forced to include a number of players who simply were not ready to play for the first team, just so we met the criteria.

That year, though, we still had a problem. We had Jamie Carragher and Steven Gerrard, of course, as well as Jermaine Pennant, our only English first-team players. We could bolster the list with Kelly, Spearing and Steven Irwin, another young player, but we were still two short. Our transfer policy would have to centre on English players of sufficient quality to play in the Champions League.

The two targets we identified were Robbie Keane, a striker at Tottenham Hotspur, and Gareth Barry, an England international midfielder at Aston Villa. I spoke to our senior players about both, and their responses were uniformly positive. Everyone saw them as the sort of signings that would suit us perfectly.

Barry appealed to us for a number of reasons. I have never been the sort of manager who prioritises a system above all else: I am willing to change and adapt my preferred formations given the strength of my squad or the requirements of a particular game. Barry was perfect: he could play as a central midfielder, of course, but he had some experience as an attacking left-back, which would be a useful option for home games where we were expected to go forward, and even as a left-winger. People who knew him told us he was a good professional, dedicated to his career, and a fine player. His nationality and price made him the ideal signing.

At the same time, we knew we needed another striker, someone to relieve the goal-scoring burden from Fernando Torres, and a player who could act as a partner, as well as a replacement. Keane's proven record for a number of clubs made him a good candidate.

The problem, of course, as ever, was that we did not have that much money. The interest payments the Americans were giving to the banks as a result of the loans they had taken out to buy the club were eating into our transfer budget, so we had to be clever. It would be much easier if football was a case of just selling the players you no longer needed. It is not. Sometimes, you have to part with a valued asset.

We knew we would have to sell players that summer if we were to raise the funds to bring in the reinforcements – and, in particular, the British reinforcements – we needed. That would require parting company with one of our current squad members who would fetch a substantial fee. We decided that the most likely candidate was Xabi Alonso, who had been a great player for us since we signed him from Real Sociedad, but had not quite performed to his best in the last couple of years. He remained coveted on the continent and we knew we had to make a sacrifice if we were to build the squad we needed.

Juventus – no doubt still remembering his excellent performance against them in 2005 – had shown a strong interest, but they would not meet our valuation. They did not want to pay what Alonso was worth, hoping that we would be forced to lower our estimate as the summer wore on. That was not the case: we needed a certain amount, to cover the fee for Barry and give us some funds in reserve for other players. We could not afford to sell cheap.

The deal to sign Keane was rather more straightforward. Negotiations progressed smoothly, and confirmation of his signing sent a wave of confidence around the club. Everyone was delighted, the staff and the players, that we had managed to land one of our prime targets.

Negotiations with Aston Villa over Barry were much slower going, though. We could not agree a fee that we felt was suitable and it became increasingly clear there was little or no chance that a deal would be completed. At almost the same time as we made it plain to Juventus that they would have to meet our valuation if they wanted to sign Alonso, we pulled out of talks with Villa.

We managed to land another target to play at left-back – the Italian Andrea Dossena, from Udinese – but Alonso, aware that he had been available, would have to stay.

The issue was still dragging on as we prepared for our Champions League qualifying tie against Standard Liege of Belgium. It was the worst draw we could possibly have been given: as ever, they were slightly further ahead in their season than us and we had lost Lucas and Javier Mascherano for a month after they requested permission to play in the Olympic Games, in Beijing, for Brazil and Argentina.

We travelled to Belgium with just four central midfielders: Steven Gerrard, who was being troubled by a lower back injury, the young players Jay Spearing and Damien Plessis, and Alonso. My plan was to play Plessis, a strong, athletic midfielder, alongside my countryman. We could not risk Gerrard. I outlined it to the players in our hotel, but after I had finished speaking, Xabi asked if he might have a quiet word with me.

The transfer window was still open and, after a summer of uncertainty, he was still unsure over his future. The details of that conversation must remain private, but I was certain that, in a game of such importance, there was no option but to play the best team available to us; Xabi, of course, would be part of that. As soon as we had finished talking, I sought out Rick Parry, our chief executive, and Sammy Lee, now appointed my assistant. I told them what had been said, but made it clear that Xabi would be playing the following night. The club had to come first.

Given the events of that game, it was clear we had made the right choice. Standard had a host of excellent young players – particularly Marouane Fellaini, Steven Defour and Axel Witsel in midfield – and were clearly a threat. Fellaini, who we would become very familiar with after his move to Everton, struck a post in the early exchanges, before Dossena was wrongly adjudged to have handled the ball in the box. Dante Bonfim, Standard's central defender, stepped up to take the penalty.

Yet again, we were left grateful to all of the assiduous work Xavi Valero had done in studying the opposition's spot-kick tendencies. Dante was hardly a regular taker, but we knew he had, in the past, gone to the goalkeeper's right, the ball not leaving the ground. From the touchline, Xavi desperately tried to remind Reina of his advice before the game: don't jump, just dive. Reina listened, smothering the penalty. A let-off. There would be more, as Standard missed a number of chances to take an advantage back to Anfield. We had escaped, there was no doubt about that.

The return leg, two weeks later, was just as closely fought. For all that we had been relieved to leave Belgium with a draw, we were still in a weak position. If Standard scored, we would need two simply to scrape through to the group stages. To their credit, they travelled to Anfield without any fear and were clearly intent on beating us. Reina had to be alert twice in the opening exchanges. We played with both Keane and Torres upfront, to try to stretch the game, but we struggled to break Standard down.

The clock ticked. No goals, after 180 minutes. Extra time. A penalty appeal, for a foul on Nabil El Zhar, our winger, turned down. We were edging closer and closer to a shootout, one that would cost the club millions if we lost. We were always confident, thanks to Xavi Valero and to Reina, but there are no certainties in such situations. Usually so noisy, so buoyant on European nights, Anfield was nervous, quiet.

And then, with just two minutes, only 120 seconds, to go, Ryan Babel turned back on himself on the left wing and sent a deep cross to the far post, over all of Standard's defenders. Kuyt met the ball with a volley, cracking his shot in low to the goalkeeper's right. All those nerves, all that tension, were released in one, single, jubilant cheer. We were through. It had been close, but we were through to the group stages. Yet again, Europe was testing the full range of our emotions: fear, despair, anxiety and sheer, unbridled delight.

The goal that gave me most pleasure when we opened our group stage campaign with a 2–1 win at Marseille was not, surprisingly, the wonderful, volleyed effort from Steven Gerrard which cancelled out Lorik Cana's opener for the French team, but the penalty our captain converted a few minutes later. Not because he had to retake it, displaying a cool head and an absence of nerves in doing so, but because of the way the foul was won by Ryan Babel.

We worked ceaselessly with Babel after we signed him from Ajax in the summer of 2007, spending hours and hours with him on the training pitch. He had abundant natural talent – that is what had attracted us to him in the first place – but too often he was let down by an inability to make the right decision.

Despite being predominantly right-footed, we were playing him on the left wing, where we thought he could make best use of his searing pace, his technical ability and his explosive shot. It was a slightly different position for him, one that required a little fine-tuning: at Ajax, he had played as a left-sided attacker in a 4–3–3, but in our 4–2–3–1, wide left was the obvious place to use him.

The problem was that he constantly chose to cut in on his right-hand side whenever he received possession. A winger has two choices: to go outside or to come in. If you do either one too often, defenders come to know what to expect. You make their lives significantly easier. Babel always came in. Both in the Premier League and in Europe, teams knew what he was likely to do, nullifying him as a threat.

We went through a host of exercises trying to change that. I would stand in the middle of the training pitch with him, playing him dozens, hundreds, of passes, aimed at one or both of his feet. I would tell him that if he used his right foot to control the ball, he should use his acceleration and his speed, get to the byline and cross; if it arrived on his left, then he could come inside. I even came up with a mantra – if you have space, use your pace – to help him remember.

It is the manager's job to improve his players, to teach them the fundamental principles, the basic movements they need to make the most of their ability. That is what I understand by man-management: individually tailoring your training to strengthen the weakest areas of their game.

And it was the product of all of that work which led to that penalty: Babel controlled a long pass from Carragher on his right foot, shimmied, moved it on to his left and skipped past Ronald Zubar, the full-back, who brought him down. Our efforts were starting to pay off.

Gerrard eventually scored the penalty to give us a lead we had deserved, after making a number of chances in the opening few minutes, and that would be enough to secure victory.

Our next game pitted us against increasingly familiar opposition: yet again, we were drawn with PSV Eindhoven in the group stages. It would be the third time we played them at home and away in my time at Liverpool. Not once did we lose to them, beating them at Anfield 3–1, in a victory that included a first Champions League goal for Robbie Keane.

He would get his second three weeks later, in possibly our hardest fixture, away at Atlético Madrid. The Vicente Calderón is an imposing stadium, its stands steep and full, its noise impressive. The atmosphere, in fact, is not unlike Anfield: the fans share the same sort of deep-seated passion. Whatever the circumstances, it is a difficult prospect, and that night, sadly, we were without our first-choice striker, absent through injury.

That was a particular shame for Torres, who had been desperate to play in the fixture. Along with Alonso, Reina and Alvaro Arbeloa, Torres had made history the previous summer, scoring the goal that beat Germany in the final of the European Championships and earned Spain its first major football trophy for more than forty years. He came back to Melwood, after an extended break, three inches taller, such was his pride. They all did. He had wanted to go back not just to his homeland and the city where he grew up, but to his old club too, the one he had supported all of his life, to show them what he had become since leaving.

He had a point to prove, after all: the press in Spain is broadly split between those newspapers that support Real Madrid and those that back Barcelona. Torres, an Atlético fan and the club's captain, had always fallen between the two camps, neither perhaps giving him the credit he deserved. This was his chance to prove to them that, a European champion now, he had not let their disregard damage his development, and it was a considerable blow that he would have to remain at Melwood to receive treatment for his injury and would therefore miss the tie.

It was for just these circumstances, though, that we had wanted to draft in an alternative, someone who could cover for Torres when he was unavailable. Keane scored early on in the game, temporarily quieting the Calderón, before Simao Sabrosa – another familiar face – scored a late equaliser.

The roles would be reversed at Anfield, when Atlético – again facing a team without Torres – went in at half-time in the lead, thanks to a goal from Maxi Rodríguez. He was one of several extremely talented players in the Spanish team, including Diego Forlán and Sergio Aguero, and they played that night like a side capable of beating anyone in Europe. Only at the very end did we equalise; indeed, it was five minutes into injury time when Gerrard won and converted a penalty to ensure we remained unbeaten in the competition.

We secured top place in the group – and the slight advantage of playing the second leg of our last sixteen tie at home – with two consecutive victories in our two remaining games. A goal from Gerrard was enough to make sure there was no repeat of Marseille's shock victory at Anfield the year before, no nervous wait to see if we had qualified, before we again beat PSV 3–1, this time in Holland. That night brought a first goal in Europe for David Ngog, a young French striker we had signed very cheaply from Paris Saint-Germain.

He was often criticised, Ngog, in his early games with us, but we knew he had pace and was technically a very good player. The problem, of course, was that ordinarily he appeared as a substitute for Torres, our superstar and the source of many of our goals. It is a daunting task to fill such imposing boots.

We had tasted defeat just once in the Premier League by the time the draw for the last sixteen of the Champions League paired us with Real Madrid in mid-December. That had been a loss at Tottenham, thanks to an injury-time goal from the Russian striker Roman Pavlyuchenko, in a game we dominated. We created opportunity after opportunity to extend our lead after Dirk Kuyt, in the third minute, had put us ahead, but the ball simply would not cross the line. On another day, we might have won by three or four goals. As it was, in his first game in charge at White Hart Lane, Harry Redknapp earned the most fortunate of victories. As we shook hands after the game, he looked at me, a baffled smile on his face, and shrugged his shoulders. He did not know how they had managed to beat us either.

That would be just one of two defeats that season in the Premier League, as we fought for the title with Manchester United. The other would not come until March, at Middlesbrough, when an injury to Alvaro Arbeloa forced me to play Martin Skrtel at right-back. We had no choice but to use him in that unfamiliar position because of the circumstances we found ourselves in. It was the best we could do.

It was our best league campaign in my time at Liverpool, even if it did come against a backdrop of strife at the club. The relationship with our two American owners was now almost entirely broken down, their presence rarely felt at Anfield and the protests against their continued ownership growing more and more vociferous in the stands. Tom Hicks had decided he did not wish to work with Rick Parry and, by the end of that season, had forced his resignation. The debt was mounting and we knew we did not have much money to spend.

All we could do was to encourage the players to forget about everything else that was going on and concentrate on making sure there was enough going on on the pitch to cheer up the fans. Of course, the senior members of the squad were concerned about what was going on between the owners. I would speak with them all regularly, to share whatever I knew, to assuage their fears and, most of all, to prove to them that my focus had not waned. If they can see that you are concentrating, that your mind is on your job, then they are more likely to follow your example.

Their performances that year suggested they were more than capable of putting all of the uncertainty, all of the chaos, out of their minds. We beat Manchester United at Anfield in September and, in October, became the first team to win at Chelsea in four years. By early December, we were top of the table. I should have been sleeping easily. I was not. In fact, I was not sleeping at all.

I had noticed a growing pain in my kidney that meant it was agony simply to lie down. Montse encouraged me to go to the hospital. They told me I had a kidney stone, and required an operation.

'Couldn't I just drink some water and take some painkillers?' I asked.

No, came the reply. The stone was too large. It would have to be removed.

'When?'

'Tomorrow.'

The next day, I went in for surgery. It was a success. I was told to rest at home for a few days. Still, though, it was difficult to sleep. I could not lie down, so had to resort to drifting off while sitting in a chair. Back we went to the hospital. More tests, more scans, using a dye to help them see what was wrong with my kidney on the X-rays. I had to wait forty minutes for the results, and was kept company by a kindly nurse, who tried to distract me by telling me that her daughter was also suffering from kidney problems and was about to receive a transplant from her boyfriend. It was a touching story, but perhaps not one to be told before I got the results from the scan on my own kidney. I did not even want to consider that I might need a transplant!

The results came back. I had a hole in my kidney. Maybe the stone had been broken during the course of the earlier operation. I would need to go under the knife, as the newspapers say, once more.

'When?'

'Tomorrow.'

As I was being wheeled into the theatre once more, I struck up a conversation with the porter. He told me he had bet on Liverpool to win the previous week and had lost. Worse was to come, though: he informed me he was an Evertonian. That was the last thing I needed to hear as the anaesthetic started to kick in, to know that there was a fan of our oldest rivals in the room, and one who felt I owed him money.

All went well, though. They inserted a stent and told me it would need to stay in for fifteen days and that, in the meantime, I was to continue resting. I had already missed one game, at Arsenal, receiving updates on the phone from Xavi Valero, the goalkeeping coach, and would have to watch our game at Newcastle from the stands.

The journey to St James's Park is a long one and, after two kidney operations, a very uncomfortable one. I took my place in the directors' box, with plenty of water and packets of painkillers on hand. We were leading 2–0 just before the interval and, in my weakened state, I knew I would have to leave early if I was to get to the dressing room for half-time. Only when I arrived did the players tell me that it was 2–1. Newcastle had pulled a goal back as I gingerly made my way down the stairs. The quick changes to my plans that I made did not seem to affect us too much, though, as we ran out 5–1 winners, guaranteeing that we would end the calendar year on top of the Premier League and on course for our first title for twenty years.

By the time I returned to work, I was ready to try to apply a little more pressure to our nearest challengers and greatest threat, Manchester United. We were playing well, in a rich vein of form, and reports reached me that the mood in Sir Alex Ferguson's camp was not the greatest. They had a hugely important game with Chelsea the following weekend, while we would travel to Stoke, a difficult fixture, but one I felt we could win. We had an opportunity to turn the screw a little, perhaps to tempt them into making a rare mistake.

I was calm as I entered the press-conference room at Melwood. I fielded one or two questions from Sky, who always go first in those pre-match briefings, and then pulled a piece of paper from my jacket pocket. I kept my voice level, objective, and read from my notes a list of facts: about Ferguson, about United, about how they behaved with referees, about their unfounded complaints over the fixture list.

'I am not talking about my impression, but things everybody can see every single week. I have been here for five years and I know what is going on.' I talked about the scheduling of fixtures, of Ferguson's criticism of referees, and joked that Chelsea should keep an eye on his coaching staff, who were constantly trying to pressurise the match officials.

'If he wants to talk about fixtures, and have a level playing field, as you say in England, there are two options. One is the same as in Spain: the draw for the first half of the league is known, and in the second half everyone plays the opposite, so you all know. Or there is another option: that Mr Ferguson organises the fixtures in his office and sends it to us and everyone will know and not complain. That is simple.

'We know what happens every time we go to Old Trafford. Chelsea need to use the zonal marking system against the staff of United because they are always [chatting] man to man with the referees when they go to the bench. Especially at half-time, they are always walking close to the referees and talking. So for all the managers, they need to know only Mr Ferguson can talk about fixtures, referees and nothing happens.'

That speech, made in a relaxed voice and with a little humour, was described, in the weeks to come, as a 'rant', as the moment when Ferguson's mind-games started to trouble me, as the beginning of the end of our title challenge. That makes a good story for the media, of course, and such an image appeals in particular to Manchester United fans.

The numbers, though, do not bear that theory out: we would win eleven games between that press conference and the end of the season. The majority of foreign players do not read the press, and I am confident that they were not affected by such things. We were really focused on our task. The more significant issue – but perhaps the less interesting story – is that United had two games in hand. They won both, allowing them to whittle down our lead.

That, more than Ferguson's psychological games, was the deciding factor. I had long known the way the United manager worked, and I never really let his words get to me. Each manager goes about the job in the manner they deem appropriate. It was not the case that I was cracking up, as the United fans sang to me, or losing my focus. It was simply an attempt to gain an advantage for my team, to see if United could cope with a little extra pressure. They did – their run of form to win the title was outstanding. We would give them one final scare, though, before the season was out, one that would live long in the memory.

25 February 2009: Real Madrid 0–1 Liverpool

Real Madrid: Casillas; Sergio Ramos, Pepe, Cannavaro, Heinze; Robben, L Diarra, Gago, Marcelo (Guti, 46); Higuaín, Raúl
Liverpool: Reina; Arbeloa, Skrtel, Carragher, Aurelio; Alonso, Mascherano; Kuyt (Lucas, 90), Benayoun, Riera (Gerrard, 88); Torres (Babel, 61)

There is no other position befitting Liverpool. Everything else, after all, is just second or third last. That we were finally placed where we belonged was testament to all that we had done throughout our time at Anfield, all of those famous nights under the floodlights, sound-tracked by the delirious cheers of our fans, the triumphs in San Siro and Camp Nou, the steel we had shown in the Stadio Delle Alpi, the ruthless elegance witnessed in the Velodrome.

It was not something we would be awarded a trophy for achieving, but it was a huge source of pride regardless: according to UEFA's co-efficient system, our achievements over the last five years made Liverpool the highest-ranked team in Europe.

There was still one scalp we had to claim, though. One ground left to conquer.

Returning to Real Madrid for the first leg of our last sixteen tie that season, of course, was special for me. It was the club I had supported when I was growing up, the place where I had started my playing career and where I had first learned the ropes as a coach and as a manager.

It was great to be back, to be stopped by people in the streets of my home city, wishing me luck for tomorrow night's game, to see so many old friends when I arrived at the stadium twenty-four hours before kick-off to train and give a press conference. Real is that sort of club: there are people still working there today who were present when I was a player, thirty-five years ago, and when I was there as a coach, twenty-five years ago. They are good, dedicated people, and it was a pleasure to catch up with them, to renew old friendships. That would not mean anything the following day, of course. They might be my friends, people who had helped me and guided me years before, but I was still here to win.

The next day, after a brief team meeting detailing how we would deal with the threat posed by Real, we took the team out for a walk around the streets near our hotel, to help them relax, to stave off the boredom that can sometimes set in, to keep the nerves at bay. It was a pleasant spring day, a good time to have a stroll, to see the city. My fellow *Madrileños* welcomed us, offering encouragement, taking pictures. We returned in time for a light lunch, and then the players would go off to their rooms for an hour or two to rest.

As we were eating, my phone beeped. A text message from a friend.

'There's a rumour that you're not Liverpool manager any more,' it read.

I looked around. I was wearing a club tracksuit, eating lunch with Steven Gerrard, Fernando Torres, Pepe Reina and the rest of the squad. If I wasn't Liverpool manager any more, nobody had thought to tell me.

It continued throughout the afternoon. A steady trickle of messages from staff members, friends, colleagues and journalists, all trying to find out if the rumour was true, that I had either resigned or been sacked by the owners, depending on which version they had heard. I did not reply to any of them. In hindsight, perhaps, that did not help the situation.

I was told that evening, after the game, that the whispers had been growing in volume throughout the day, at home and in Madrid. The club had, for some reason, not quashed it as soon as they heard it, simply meeting journalists' enquiries with a mysterious 'no comment'. The rumour grew and grew, spiralling out of control. It was all over the internet, being pursued by reporters at home and in Spain, being discussed among the thousands of fans who had made the journey to Madrid and were enjoying the build-up to the game in the sun-drenched plazas of my home city.

I assume the players heard it, some of them, as they were resting in their rooms. They did not need to do much to check, though. They only needed to knock on my door to see if it was true. By the time we drove the short distance to the Bernabéu, there was as much interest in whether I would be on the touchline as there was in which players would be selected for the game.

To this day, I have no idea where the rumours came from. At that time, relations with the owners were strained, that is true, and there were many things that needed changing behind the scenes. We were talking about a new contract and there were a number of issues that we disagreed on. That is how chaotic things were at Liverpool at the time, that on the day of the most important game of the season so far, there could be a rumour that the manager had left or been sacked, and nobody was prepared to dismiss it out of hand.

At no point, though, was there any thought in my mind about resigning, and it would have been a very strange time for them to wish to change manager: in the middle of a title race, on the day of a Champions League game against the most decorated team in European history.

There was certainly no way I would allow such rumours to distract me from finalising my preparations for the game. Real were not opponents to be taken lightly. I spent that afternoon watching DVDs of their recent games, making sure we would be able to cope with whatever they threw at us.

As ever, they had quite an arsenal. Their attack was centred around the skilful Raúl and the powerful Gonzalo Higuaín, their threat in midfield came from Arjen Robben – an old friend from our ties with Chelsea in previous years – and their defence, marshalled by the veteran Fabio Cannavaro, another familiar face, protected the goal of Iker Casillas, the Spanish national team goalkeeper. Formidable foes and, according to the Spanish press in the build-up to the game, the finest squad assembled at my old club for some considerable time. Under Juande Ramos, Real were pushing Barcelona for the Spanish league title and their domestic form was ominous.

We knew how to cope with such opponents, of course. We had done it time and again in Europe, as borne out by our UEFA ranking. We would be without Gerrard that night – still not fully fit after an injury – but we had confidence nevertheless.

The key would be to shut down Robben, to prevent him drifting in from the right-hand side to play penetrating passes or to shoot with his stronger left foot. By closing him off, we would cut off the supply line to Raúl and Higuaín. As ever, we determined not to play too deep a defensive line, so as to ensure we did not invite pressure on ourselves. We knew we would have to press them well, particularly in the wide areas. We were to look for Torres running behind the defenders, who, like so many, simply could not match him for pace. Words like 'narrow' and 'compact' may seem repetitive, but that is the way to play, especially away from home, in Europe. To have any hope of winning, it is imperative to deny your opponents space.

The Bernabéu, when full, is an impressive sight. The stands are perilously steep, and so the noise seems to wash down onto the pitch. To the left of the technical areas, Real's *ultras*, their most committed fans, wave their banners, sing their anthems and whistle, deafeningly loudly, every time their opponents have the ball. It is revered as one of the most iconic stadiums in Europe for good reason.

That night, we tamed it.

Our performance was calmly, coolly professional. The players, lined up in that familiar 4–2–3–1, closed down well, retained their shape and did not allow the movement of Real's strikers to pull them from position. Our midfield, directed and controlled by Javier Mascherano and Xabi Alonso, played close to our defensive line, shutting off all space. On the left, Fabio Aurelio and our Spanish winger Albert Riera kept a watchful eye on Robben. Every time he tried to come inside to cause damage, he would be surrounded by two or three players. Soon, we were in control.

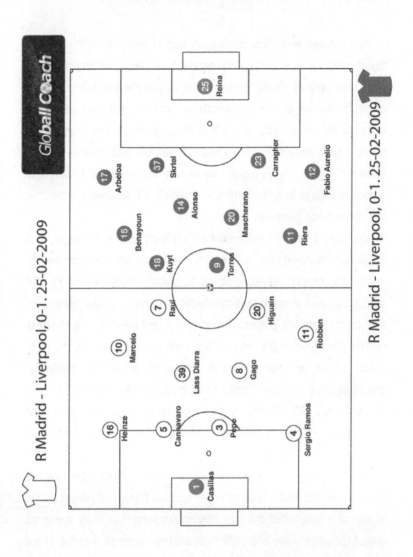

Real's most dangerous player was the Dutch winger Arjen Robben. Fabio Aurelio and Albert Riera, who would be facing him that night, knew they would have to be watchful so that he could not cut inside and shoot; Alonso and Mascherano, too, would have to play close to the defensive line to deny Real space to exploit.

Both Torres and Yossi Benayoun had chances to score on the counter-attack, and in the dressing room at half-time, my message was clear: keep on doing the same things and the breakthrough will come. It was not until eight minutes before the end that we would be rewarded for our display. By that stage, perhaps, Real might have thought they were safe. Torres had hobbled off with an ankle injury, to be replaced by Ryan Babel, unable to prove his point to the fans who had always been so hard on him while he was with Atlético – but we had not given up.

We won a free kick wide on Real's left-hand side, our right, and Fabio Aurelio stood over it. These moments are practised constantly in training, certain players dashing to certain places, trying to find the split second of space that can throw off a marker. Yossi Benayoun, one of the smallest players in our squad and possibly the shortest on the pitch that night, was tasked with making a run to the near post. Aurelio, an expert in such situations, found him perfectly: the ball glanced off the Israeli's head, past Casillas, and into the net. The Bernabéu, 80,000 strong, fell silent, except for a small pocket of our supporters high in the stands above the goal where Benayoun had scored.

We had already beaten Chelsea, Barcelona, both Inter and AC Milan, Juventus and a host of other famous European names. Now, as our fans serenaded the Real Madrid supporters as they streamed out of the ground, we had added yet another name to that list. There were no worlds left to conquer.

10 March 2009: Liverpool 4–0 Real Madrid

Liverpool: Reina; Arbeloa, Skrtel, Carragher, Aurelio; Alonso (Lucas, 60), Mascherano; Kuyt, Gerrard (Spearing, 74), Babel; Torres (Dossena, 83)
Real Madrid: Casillas; Sergio Ramos, Pepe, Cannavaro (van der Vaart, 65), Heinze; L Diarra, Gago (Guti, 77); Robben (Marcelo, 60), Sneijder; Raúl, Higuaín

The return leg was, I think, the finest European performance of my six years at Liverpool. We showed tremendous discipline to hold Juventus in 2005, and great passion and commitment to beat Chelsea that season and in 2007, while quieting Lionel Messi and Ronaldinho at Camp Nou is also a source of great pride. But that night, as we tore Madrid to shreds, we were almost perfect.

It was not supposed to be that way. As the day of the return leg approached, the Spanish press began to highlight quite how confident Real were. Vicente Boluda, then the club's president, suggested the game would be a *chorreo* – literally, a cascade, a waterfall. The inference is clear: in England, perhaps, he would have said that his side would sweep us away. The day before the match, *Marca*, a newspaper based in Madrid, published a front-page piece declaring: *Esto es Anfield, y que?* This is Anfield – so what?

Some managers would use such articles, such over-confidence on the part of the opposition, as inspiration for their players, but that can be counter-productive, especially when translation from another language is required. All of our Spanish players were well aware of what had been said and what had been written about the game, though, and they would have passed the message on to the rest of the squad. We did not have those quotes up in the dressing room, but we knew Real were confident they would over-turn that first-leg deficit. And we were certain they had a nasty shock in store.

My key message in the dressing room before the game was that we had to deprive Real of any hope whatsoever. We wanted to start fast, intense, be on top of them from the very first whistle. We needed to show them that they were in for a night they would want to forget. They knew they had to attack, to score: the sooner we could convince them that they would not, the sooner they would lose confidence.

'We have to be intense,' I told the players, after naming the team and before leaving them to listen to music, to have a quick massage, to talk with each other, or to finalise their roles in set pieces. 'Stick together, be unified. Especially in the early minutes, try to get the ball quickly. Right on top of them, as soon as they have possession. Don't give them so much as a second to play a pass or to keep the ball. Don't allow them time. Don't allow them any hope that they can come here and win.'

Our idea in such games was normally to press the ball high, but against Madrid we made a slight alteration: we would allow their central defenders a little bit of possession, encourage them to come forward with the ball. Only once they approached the halfway line would we begin to press. That way, if we won the ball back, there would be space to run into, particularly for Torres, returned from

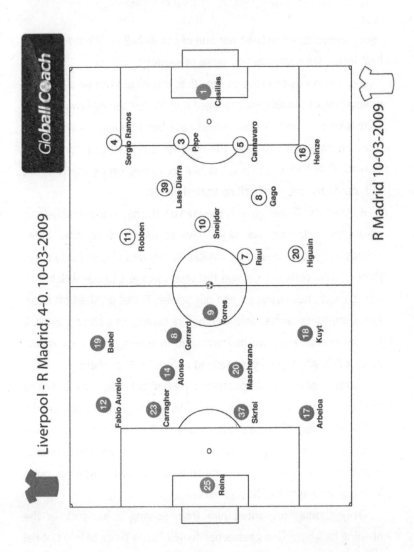

Though the quality in Real's line-up was high, our plan was to be as intense as possible from the start to make them realise the scale of the task facing them. We would, though, allow Pepe and Cannavaro a little possession, so as to draw their defensive line higher and create more space for Torres.

injury and restored to the front line of our 4–2–3–1. We were to lull Real into a false and fleeting sense of security.

If our aim was to prove to Real that this would not be a *chorreo*, or anything of the sort, we managed it in those opening few minutes. That is when Juande Ramos would have been hoping his side could score an early goal, to level the tie once more, to test our nerves. Instead, Real barely touched the ball as, roared on by the Kop, we swarmed forward, pummelling their defence.

By the time Torres gave us the lead on the night and doubled our advantage in the tie, we might have scored twice or three times already, only to be denied by Casillas. When we did eventually break through their resistance, it was testament not just to our skill, but to our strength, our character and our power: Torres brushed off Pepe, Real's imposing central defender, before turning in a cross from Dirk Kuyt. It was a move we had practised in training, the movements now drilled into the players, second nature to all of them.

Torres, that night, was possessed. He had been denied the chance to play against Atlético, his former side, in the group stages, and he had been forced off from the Bernabéu with an ankle injury. He was determined to make up for lost time. He seemed desperate to remind everyone in his homeland how much he had grown as a player, quite how powerful a striker he had become.

Only Casillas prevented him from scoring a hat-trick in the opening half-hour. The goalkeeper denied Torres twice before Gabriel Heinze was adjudged to have handled the ball in the area and, despite Real's appeals, Gerrard stepped up and scored from the penalty spot.

At half-time, the players were bristling with confidence and pride. In those moments when everything seems impossible or victory distant, it is important that the manager's message is one of hope, of calm, of belief. When things are going so well, it is crucial that the players do not get carried away, that they are reminded that – whatever the score – they must focus completely for ninety minutes, especially against opponents as talented and dangerous as Real Madrid. It is not a case of bringing the players down or not enjoying their performance, but of making sure they concentrate for the rest of the game. 'Stay compact and narrow in defence,' I told them, 'and keep pressing. Don't give Madrid a minute.'

Within 120 seconds of the interval, any hope our visitors might have had of an unlikely comeback had disappeared entirely. Yet again, Ryan Babel showed how far he had come, how much he had learned from those hours on the training field, improving his crossing, making sure he did not always cut inside and dribble into a crowd of players. He escaped down the left wing and crossed, low, into the box. Gerrard, as ever, was charging into the area. He met it with the side of his foot and the ball shot high into the Kop net. Perhaps there would be a *chorreo* after all, but maybe not the sort that would delight Sr Boluda.

The score-line would, undoubtedly, have been more emphatic had we been facing any other goalkeeper in the world – apart, perhaps, from our very own Pepe Reina, largely an impressed spectator that night as his team-mates flooded forwards. Casillas denied Gerrard, then Torres again. The ball rarely left Madrid's half. Almost every attack seemed to end in a shot, in a chance, each one greeted with applause from the rapturous Kop. In the end, it would be an unlikely hero who added the final *coup de grace* – Andrea Dossena, a late substitute, beating Casillas late on.

I was delighted for Dossena, who had not settled well in England. His dedication to the club, to proving he was not a bad signing, that he could be a success, was impressive. His fitness regime was hugely demanding, and when he was not playing, he simply asked more of himself. More hours on the treadmill, more sessions in the gym. Here, at last, after a difficult season, was a moment he could enjoy.

We were applauded off, long and loud, by Anfield that night. So, too, was Casillas. The European Championship-winning goalkeeper was in tears, so heavy was the defeat his side had suffered. It was a generous gesture from our supporters, and one he deserved: after all, he had been awarded Man of the Match for his efforts. The damage could have been much, much worse had he not been at the very top of his form that night.

The praise we received in the subsequent days for our performance, for the manner in which we had humbled one of the best teams in the world, was lavish. One view, in particular, was heartening. Zinedine Zidane, the former France international and one of the finest players in Real's rich history, was so impressed by Gerrard's performance that night that he went as far as describing our captain as the best player in the world.

That was testament to all of Gerrard's hard work, of course, but it was a source of tremendous pride for me as his manager too: all of the hours we had put in on the training ground, altering aspects of his game, encouraging him to do certain things, changing his position, had all helped him fulfil his tremendous potential. Now, he stood among the great of the world game.

I always like to improve my players, wherever I can. It was the same for Jamie Carragher. When we arrived, he was a perfectly capable but unspectacular left-back, the position given to him by my predecessor, Gerard Houllier. We helped turn him into one of the best central defenders in Europe. That is one of the parts of the manager's job that I enjoy the most: the opportunity to help develop players, to educate them, and to see them grow. That night against Madrid was the culmination of all of that work, the night when the two local boys from Huyton and Bootle made the world sit up and take notice.

We were not yet finished. Our week would have a golden ending.

Four days later, on a sunny Saturday lunchtime at Old Trafford, we did to Manchester United what we had done to Real Madrid. It was the biggest victory Liverpool had recorded at the home of their old enemies for seventy years. It blew the Premier League title race open once more and sent a shockwave through England. The reigning champions, the dominant force of the last two decades, dismantled at home, humiliated by four goals to one.

Our game-plan centred on Nemanja Vidic, United's centre-back. Vidic played on the left-hand side of Sir Alex Ferguson's defence, despite being right-footed, alongside the attack-minded left-back Patrice Evra. Mirroring what we had done against Real, we intended to allow Vidic possession in his own half, not pressing him early, so that he might come forward with the ball. Evra, at the same time, would start his run forward. As soon as we regained possession, Torres was to target the space the two defenders, now out of position, had vacated.

That is precisely how we earned both of our two goals before half-time, a strike from Torres which cancelled out Cristiano Ronaldo's penalty and a spot-kick of our own, won and converted by Steven Gerrard.

We extended our lead at a crucial time in the second half, Fabio Aurelio whipping a free kick past Edwin van der Sar just as Ferguson was about to make three substitutions in an attempt to take control of the game. Dossena, spectacularly, added a fourth in injury time. United looked shell-shocked, our fans disbelieving. We had humbled the champions on their own territory.

As the players celebrated in the dressing room, I climbed the stairs to the media suite at Old Trafford. I had a message I wanted to convey: not one of disrespect to United, far from it, but one to the rest of the league, who we knew could help us in our bid to win our first title for two decades. I wanted to prove to them that, with good players and a clear game-plan, it was possible to beat Manchester United, even at Old Trafford. They were not invincible.

'We knew their defence had weaknesses,' I said, trying to remain calm, to make my points so that other teams might copy our blueprint. All the talk of rants, about our team losing its focus and crumbling under pressure, had disappeared now. 'When they don't have the ball and you move the ball quickly and play behind their defenders, you know you can beat them. We had to go forward quickly because they are an offensive team and they are always high up the pitch. We knew that with Torres's movement, we could create problems for their defenders.'

If just one or two of our counterparts copied our plan and had a little luck, they could help us beat United to the Premier League title. All we could do was keep up the pressure. We did that, emphatically, the following week, routing Aston Villa 5–0 at Anfield. They may not have quite the same resonance around the world as Real Madrid, but that was a strong Villa team, under Martin O'Neill, a side in contention for a Champions League place. We simply blew them away.

That fortnight, in which we twice beat Madrid, humiliated our fiercest rivals and then comprehensively overcame Villa, may have been the best two weeks of my time at Liverpool, Istanbul apart. We produced four stunning performances against top-quality opposition. It was a tremendous achievement, and one we hoped would bring us at least one of the two trophies we desired most come the end of the season.

It was not to be. We dropped just two more points in the league that season, in that breathless, bewitching 4–4 draw with Arsenal at Anfield, concluding the campaign with five straight wins to reach a club record total of eighty-six points in a thirty-eight-game season. We had scored more goals, too, than we had ever managed in the Premier League era.

In most years, it would have been enough to win the title. United, though, despite defeat at Fulham, came back from losing positions against both Villa and Tottenham. They simply did not drop enough points. The run of form they produced to win the championship, drawing level with Liverpool's record of eighteen titles, was hugely impressive, but that did not temper our immense disappointment. We had come so close to ending Liverpool's long, long wait for a championship. We failed by the slenderest of margins.

Our Champions League campaign ended in similar circumstances. Our reward for conquering the Bernabéu was to find Chelsea yet again barring our path, this time at the quarter-final stage. Our opponents, once more, were in a state of flux: Luiz Felipe Scolari, the man appointed to replace Avram Grant, had departed in February after we had beaten his side 2–0 at Anfield in the Premier League, to be replaced by Guus Hiddink until the end of the season.

Hiddink had galvanised the team – he would end his brief stay by lifting the FA Cup – but we were, for once, favourites going into the tie. After all, it was Liverpool, not Chelsea, hunting down Manchester United for the league title, and it was Liverpool, not Chelsea, who looked a fearsome, well-oiled, smooth-running machine.

We played that role well for much of the first half of our first leg. Fernando Torres scored after just six minutes and, for a moment, it appeared we would swat Chelsea aside, teeing up a semi-final against Pep Guardiola's Barcelona.

A few minutes before the interval, though, Branislav Ivanovic powerfully headed home from a corner, to draw the scores level and give Chelsea a crucial away goal. Ten minutes after the break, he scored again, in strikingly similar circumstances. When Didier Drogba scored a third, we knew we faced an almost impossible task to reach the last four.

The next day, once again, we found our zonal-marking system was the victim of scathing criticism. Just as we had for years, though, we defended in a far more sophisticated fashion. It is always important to adapt your marking strategy to the opposition; we knew Ivanovic was strong in the air, so we detailed one of our central defenders to pick him up, man-to-man. The problem was not the system, it was that there was nobody blocking the Serb's run, nobody jumping with him. Zonal marking, man-to-man marking, a mixture of the two: all can be effective, but there is no system in existence that is not vulnerable to simple human error.

That defeat meant that, when we travelled to Stamford Bridge the following week, we knew we had to attack. We would need to score three times to qualify, at a ground where Chelsea had suffered just a handful of defeats in the last five years. 'There's no rush,' I told the players before the game. 'We need one goal, then another goal, and then we are in the game.'

Within thirty minutes, most Liverpool fans could scarcely believe their eyes. We were leading by two goals to nil. We had come back from the dead. First, Fabio Aurelio had caught Petr Cech out with a clever free kick, shooting from thirty-five yards out after he had shaped to cross the ball. Then Xabi Alonso converted a penalty. Perfect. We were just a goal away from the semi-finals.

'We have to be careful,' I reminded the squad at half-time. I feared that the Spanish referee would penalise the slightest physical contact, and the events at Anfield six days earlier had proved that Chelsea could be a threat from set pieces. 'No free kicks. No fouls. Don't give them chances.'

We conceded in the most unfortunate of circumstances, Drogba touching a cross from Nicolas Anelka on to Reina, who could not quite stop the ball going in. Then Alex, the Brazilian defender, scored direct from a free kick: the referee awarded twenty-nine fouls against us that night. We were not careful enough. When we went 3–2 down, to a goal from Frank Lampard, Chelsea must have thought our resistance was finished.

Not quite.

First, Lucas drew us level on the night with a deflected effort, and then, a minute later, Dirk Kuyt gave us the lead with a header. There were eight minutes left. Stamford Bridge fell silent, except for our fans, jubilant, disbelieving. One more goal and we would go through. We had no choice but to push forward. There is an element of risk at such times, of course. It is natural to gamble. We were attempting a comeback almost as unlikely as Istanbul. Chelsea caught us on the counter-attack. 4–4. It was over. We were out of the Champions League.

We had departed in style, though. We had departed with another reminder to Europe that Liverpool never give up – no matter how difficult the circumstances – without a fight.

The following day, the entire squad boarded the bus at Melwood for the short drive to Anfield. As every year, a service would be held at the stadium to commemorate the anniversary of the Hillsborough disaster, in which ninety-six Liverpool fans lost their lives. 2009 marked twenty years since that dark day, and, whereas ordinarily only the Kop is opened, the club, expecting a far larger turnout of mourners than usual, had decided to open the entire ground. More than 30,000 people attended the ceremony, each one present to pay their respects to those who went to a football match and never came home.

It is a solemn, sombre occasion, one in which the club shows that it is more than a business, more than a football team; it is an institution that belongs to a wider community, to the city.

But as the squad walked from the tunnel, heads bowed in reverence, towards the Kop, a ripple of applause rang round the stadium, followed by an impromptu chorus of 'You'll Never Walk Alone'. Nowhere else in the world would a team be able to return to its home stadium, the day after being eliminated from a competition, and be greeted by such warmth on an occasion of such sadness.

That is what marks Liverpool as special: on days like that, the fans show that they are with the team, no matter what, and the team, mourning the loss of ninety-six supporters, show that they are at one with the fans.

6

Season 2009–10
An End

FOR FIVE YEARS, I HAD BEEN A FOOTBALL MANAGER AT Liverpool. By the start of my sixth, it was clear I had become something else entirely. I was suddenly supposed to be a bank manager. The club was no longer concerned about team-sheets as much as spreadsheets, the balance of the side was not seen as important as the balance in the bank. Everything was analysed like it was a business. Decisions were being made to appease the banks, not the fans.

That is how serious the situation with the owners, Tom Hicks and George Gillett, had become.

They had been living off short-term loans, at high interest rates, for some time, and the banks who owned that debt were now growing as concerned as the fans. One of the conditions of the loan they took out that summer was the appointment of a new managing director, Christian Purslow, who was tasked with raising £100 million of investment to help alleviate the club's debt.

It was obvious straightaway who was now in charge of Liverpool, and what mattered most. I was surprised to see our managing director at the back of every press conference, at every interview I gave. I had to take him out of the dressing room and try to stop him appearing at the training ground and engaging in long conversations with players. That is not normal for a football club, and it was certainly not what I had been used to at Liverpool. It was clear that something was very wrong.

Attempting to work in the transfer market that summer was almost impossible.

We had long worked in the same way, as we tried to strengthen our squad: seeing who we could afford to buy, who we would have to sell, and establishing exactly what our budget was. It had never been too large, by the standards of many of our rivals, but it was always expressed as a net figure, the exact sum we had that we could pay in transfer fees to the clubs we were buying from. We did not have to concern ourselves with any other payments.

That summer, everything changed. We knew that we would lose Xabi Alonso, who had an offer from Real Madrid, and who had made up his mind to submit a transfer request. My friends in Spain had told me as much, and I was sure to tell the club to demand as high a price as possible when the bid eventually came. We needed all the money we could get to increase our budget.

Our choice to replace him was Alberto Aquilani, an Italian international at Roma. We wanted an offensive midfielder, someone who would be able to create more clear-cut chances for our attack, a player who would be able to provide the penetrating passes that Fernando Torres, in particular, thrived on. Lucas and Javier Mascherano would be our defensive midfield players, and Aquilani's presence, we decided, would balance the side, thanks to his mobility and his creativity.

The problem was his fitness. In truth, he was only within our price range because he had suffered an ankle injury the previous season and had been forced to undergo an operation to fix the problem. The doctor who had carried out that surgery told us that he would need one month to recover fully. We decided to get a second opinion from our own medical staff, who confidently predicted that Aquilani would return in two months.

To be safe, we sent him to Harley Street, to see an ankle specialist. He told us the injury would require three months to heal.

It left us in an almost impossible position. Three medical opinions, all worthy of respect, but each one completely and confidently different. We decided that we would go ahead with the deal, because we had enough cover in midfield to allow Aquilani to recover his fitness before he was introduced into the team, but sadly, all three of the experts we had consulted were proved wrong. It would be four months before he was truly ready to play, and even then, it was impossible to push him too much in training, as he was still hampered slightly by the after-effects of the injury.

He is often dismissed as a failure at Liverpool, but I am confident that, given time, he would have shown his quality, once he had fully recovered from his injuries, just as he did in the pre-season to the 2011–12 season.

In the summer that Aquilani first joined, we also sold Alvaro Arbeloa, who joined Alonso at Real Madrid. He was replaced by Glen Johnson, England's international right-back, who we felt would be able to give us more attacking options, as he was a more offensively-minded player than Arbeloa; not only that, he was another English name for our Champions League list.

Those four deals roughly cancelled each other out, in terms of cost, and we believed we still had more than enough money left over to bring in a striker. We had sold Robbie Keane back to Tottenham, recouping much of our initial outlay, in the preceding January, as well as selling off a number of squad players over the previous year or so. We knew we would need cover and support for Fernando Torres, as David Ngog was still developing, and we had raised the cash to find it.

The player we identified to fill that role was Stevan Jovetic, a young Montenegro forward playing for Fiorentina in Italy. The funds we thought we had available would also have stretched to another central defender, to provide cover for Jamie Carragher, Martin Skrtel and Daniel Agger: the two players we had identified were Sylvain Distin, then with Portsmouth, and West Ham's Matthew Upson, both boasting abundant Premier League experience.

Signing one of those two, plus the tall, powerful, intelligent Jovetic, would have given Liverpool the squad we needed to build on the previous year's title challenge, when we had run Manchester United so close.

Liverpool, though, was no longer a football club. It was a business. We were told, long after we had drawn up our plans, that we had spent all of the money available to us. I did not understand: we had more or less balanced our income and our expenditure that summer, and not touched the funds we had raised the previous January.

The answer came back: the figure we had been given at the start of July was not net, as it had been for all those years, and as we had every reason to expect it would be again. Suddenly, without prior warning, they had decided it was gross. That is a hugely significant difference.

I kept asking questions of Purslow, of the owners, and they would not give me answers. I could have guessed what had happened, of course, but their silence spoke volumes. The money which we wanted to use to take Liverpool on to the next level was all gone.

We did what we could. With the little money we had left, we signed Sotirios Kyrgiakos, a defender from AEK Athens. He was a reliable, enthusiastic player, one who always gave his all and, in time, would prove to be an important member of the squad, but we would be punished for the disappearance of that money – and our failure to sign Jovetic – again and again that season.

That was supposed to be our year, the season it all came together. We had done so well the previous season, getting so close to ending the club's twenty-year wait for a league title, and expectations were sky-high going into the following campaign.

In hindsight, there were hints all around us that it would be a difficult season, that nothing would go to plan. In the first few minutes of our visit to Tottenham in our first game of the Premier League season, Carragher and Skrtel were both on the ground, requiring treatment for injuries sustained when the two clashed heads as they competed for an aerial ball.

It would be that sort of game, one that we lost 2–1 to goals from two defenders, Benoit Assou-Ekotto and Sebastien Bassong, who are not exactly renowned for their prowess in attack. It would be that sort of season. Everything that could go wrong, did go wrong.

It was much the same in Europe. We had been placed as top seeds in the draw for the Champions League, thanks to our status as the top team in UEFA's co-efficient ranking, and we had been given a group including Lyon, the French champions and stalwarts of the competition, Fiorentina, competing for the first time in around a decade, and Debrecen, the Hungarian league winners.

We started in steady but unspectacular fashion, beating Debrecen 1–0 at Anfield, thanks to a goal on the stroke of half-time from Dirk Kuyt. We had recovered a little in the league, too, at that point, losing at home to Aston Villa but winning our five other games to ensure we were relatively well-placed by the end of September.

Our second Champions League game saw us travel to Florence, to Fiorentina's impressive Stadio Artemio Franchi, a sea of purple and a cauldron of noise. For years, we had taken such backdrops in our stride, silencing the crowd and subduing our opponents, no matter how daunting the challenge or famous the name. On that night, for the first time, we wilted. We did not play well, struggling to impose our rhythm on our opponents, unable to press the ball, failing to find space behind their defence. Twice, in the first half, Fiorentina scored. Twice, the man accepting the adulation of the stands was Jovetic, the very player we had identified as our key reinforcement for the summer but been told, at the last, we did not have the money to buy.

Another sign, another hint, that it would be a year to forget.

The visit of Lyon gave us a chance to restore our season to its usual course, to take control of our destiny in the group. We could only name a patched-up side, without Johnson, Aquilani and Torres, and within twenty-five minutes, Steven Gerrard, our captain, had limped off, injured. Still, we took the lead through Yossi Benayoun before half-time, and it looked as though we would be able to hold out and earn the victory we needed to make up for defeat in Florence. Indeed, Fabio Aurelio and Dirk Kuyt might both have extended our advantage, making the game and the points safe.

They could not, and with fifteen minutes or so to play, Lyon equalised. We pushed forward, looking for a winning goal, and found ourselves exposed on the counter-attack. Deep into injury time, Sidney Govou, a French international, burst forward and fed Cesar Delgado. The Argentine's strike evaded Pepe Reina. The Kop stood silenced. In the year it was supposed to come together, everything was falling apart.

We would be cursed by a late goal in the return game two weeks later too. We had recovered our confidence a little by that stage, beating Manchester United at Anfield, and we offered a resilient display in France; it was not a vintage performance, by any means, but it was one that our fans would have recognised from previous campaigns. It was the sort of showing, full of character and strength, which we had given Europe on any number of occasions over the past five years.

And when Ryan Babel, a substitute, picked up the ball thirty yards out, checked inside, set his body and unleashed a fizzing shot beyond the reach of Hugo Lloris, the Lyon goalkeeper, it looked like it would be enough to earn us a vital, rejuvenating victory, one that would keep our hopes of qualification alive for a little while longer. There were just seven minutes to play. We had just seven minutes to hold out.

We made three mistakes. First, Babel missed a clearing header as Lyon played a ball to the edge of our box. Instead, the ball was headed on again, over Daniel Agger, caught out of position. Then, Kyrgiakos allowed Lisandro López to wriggle past him. The Argentine finished emphatically past Reina.

In normal circumstances, a draw at Lyon would be a perfectly acceptable result. Given our desperate need for points, though, given how close we had been to victory, it was a crushing blow.

We knew now that we would have to win our final two games to have any hope at all of qualifying for the last sixteen, just as we had done in each of the previous five seasons. This time, though, we would also need help from elsewhere: we required Lyon, already qualified, to travel to Florence and avoid defeat, so that by the time Fiorentina came to Anfield for the final game of the group, we still had a chance of eliminating the Italian team.

It was not to be. On a dreadful pitch on a bitterly cold night in

Budapest, an early goal from David Ngog was all we needed to beat Debrecen, but the news from Tuscany was not good. Juan Manuel Vargas, Fiorentina's Peruvian winger, had scored a penalty midway through the first half, and the French side, with their place in the last sixteen already secured, could not find an equaliser. It was over. After five years of standing tall among Europe's elite, we would be demoted to the Europa League after Christmas.

By the time Fiorentina arrived on Merseyside in December, we knew our fate; we had nothing to play for but pride. That game, though, encapsulated our brief campaign in the Champions League that season: we took the lead just before half-time, again through Yossi Benayoun, before a goal from Martin Jorgensen drew our Italian guests level. In injury time, as the game looked destined to peter out into an unremarkable draw, Stephen Darby, our young right-back, slipped, and suddenly Fiorentina were in, Alberto Gilardino tapping home in front of their delirious fans to give them one of their most famous wins in Europe.

It was another of those games. It was one of those seasons.

The Champions League had always been a source of salvation for us, an escape, when our league form was disappointing. The previous season, after that famous victory against Real Madrid, the roles had been reversed: we were eliminated from Europe by Chelsea at the quarter-final stage, and we turned all of our energies to the Premier League title race. There is always an advantage to finding yourself out of one competition, a solace to be taken, that now, at least, you can concentrate on winning those trophies still available to you.

In my final season at Liverpool, there was no escape, no silver lining.

We were out of the Champions League, and in a fight to return to the competition the following season. Tottenham and Manchester City had both strengthened their teams considerably and had designs on taking our place in the top four. It was a long, hard campaign, a battle from start to finish.

Pressure is a vicious circle. Our fans were hoping for so much that year, and with every small problem, every injury, every dropped point, it became harder and harder to meet those expectations. That, in turn, increases the pressure on the manager, the players, everyone at the club, which simply serves to make it harder to perform. We kept pushing ourselves, pushing the squad, to get back to the level we had shown the previous year, but we just could not do it. The pressure became too much.

That is often when the problems start. Stories began to leak out that the dressing room, the players, had decided that the club needed to change its manager; that my relationship with senior members of the squad was at breaking point; that I had become too distracted by the politics of the club to pay attention to my job. All of these theories, from journalists and pundits whose interest was in protecting their friends, created a mess.

The truth is rather different. The players, the dressing room, were absolutely fine; they were disappointed by their results, but there was no sense of mutiny. It is normal that players are not happy when the team is not winning, that they are dejected when they, too, had expected so much from the season, but I am confident that every player at Liverpool that season was simply trying to do their best, to help the club return to where it had been the previous year, to make the fans' dreams come true. The likes of Javier Mascherano, Dirk Kuyt, Daniel Agger, Lucas Leiva, Glen Johnson, Martin Skrtel and Pepe Reina would not put their own self-interest above the well-being of the club. They were pushing, every second of the day, to help turn things round, and I knew I could count on their support, and that of the rest of the squad.

That is not to say that they did not know what was going on, that they could not tell that something was wrong. The playing staff, like all of us, were deeply concerned by the direction the club was taking. Most importantly, they felt they had been let down by the people in charge of the club.

The one thing players tend to want more than anything else is to see that their team is moving forward, that there are high-quality arrivals being added to the squad all the time. That is what the owners and directors of Liverpool had promised to Reina, to Torres, to Gerrard and to the others. They had been promised that money would be spent, that the squad would be strengthened. When the transfer window in August and then in January closed and the only player we had added was Maxi Rodríguez, on a free transfer, they knew something was wrong.

Of course, it is to the manager that the players turn when they have such concerns. They would regularly come to my office and ask me what was going on with the owners, complaining that promises had been broken, expressing their concerns and fears for the future of the club. The timing, particularly, hurt them: they felt we had been so close to achieving something so important the year before, and if only we had spent the money they had been told we would, perhaps we would have been able to take that final step. That is all the players wanted, particularly those who were among the finest in the world in their positions: the opportunity to win titles. They were crushed to see it slipping from our grasp because the club was being run like a business, because the filing cabinet was more important than the trophy cabinet.

Obviously, those worries and fears and doubts started to influence the mood at the club, but at no point did I notice a lack of support from the players; far from it. They knew, as I did, that we had to do better, that it is when things are difficult that you have to work harder. Instead, it was the lack of support from above that was most glaring to me.

When I first arrived at Liverpool, I had actually been quite surprised at the backing given to me by Rick Parry, the chief executive, and David Moores, the chairman, after each and every game. It was clear from the very first day that their faith was complete and the support unwavering. We had our differences at times, of course, that is only natural in such an intense environment, but they were always sure to show me that they believed in what I was doing, and that they would do everything they could to help. That feeling, that atmosphere, is crucial if a manager is to do his job to the best of his ability.

Without it, there is just a lonely chaos.

In that final year, I was under no illusions: I was entirely on my own, certainly as far as the hierarchy of the club went. I had my staff, of course, and the players, but my contact with the owners was fleeting. We would not see them for months, and we would not speak to them for weeks. I could only communicate by email, and sometimes my messages would go unanswered. Attempting to find out what was going on at Liverpool was increasingly difficult, even for the manager. The directors were not much more help. I kept asking questions. They could not give me answers.

That soon transmits to the players. They are affected by the uncertainty, just as their manager is. It creates the sort of atmosphere where any individual with an agenda can hope to influence events to their own ends, where different parties can start to agitate for whatever is in their own interests. There is no ultimate authority to put an end to it, to take control of the club, to make sure everyone is fighting for the same thing, pulling in the same direction.

In the newspapers, it was written that I had become distracted by the endless power struggles, that I was attempting to strengthen my own position in the battle with the owners, that I was more interested in playing politics than in playing football, that the team had suffered because I was not paying sufficient attention to my day job.

That could not be further from the truth. The previous season, the situation at the club had been just as confused, just as troubling, and we had come within one or two late goals of overhauling Manchester United and winning the Premier League title. Even more importantly, there is only one way to react when things are not going well on the pitch and off it, and that is to make sure that everything you can control, you do control.

I was more focused that season, I think, than I had been in any of the previous years. I knew how much harder everything would be with such a dysfunctional set-up above me, so I knew I had to do everything to the best of my abilities; I had to be a better manager that year than I had ever been before. I analysed every game even more forensically, prepared each training session in minute detail, considered every possible situation we could find ourselves facing and made sure we had an answer, a response.

The lack of support, though, was fatal. We tried all we could, we worked harder than ever, but we simply could not change the mood around the club, instil some confidence back into players who felt that Liverpool was nothing but a succession of empty promises. I did all I could to persuade the squad, to convince them to keep fighting, to make sure we were all working towards the same goal, but without the people above me doing the same, it was an uphill struggle. There were so many conflicting messages coming out of the club that it was hard for them to know which way to turn. All we wanted was for everyone to pull in the same direction. It was clear that, upstairs, they had rather different targets. The players, the fans and the staff could sense that, feel that lack of cohesion. We could not, in the boot room, make up for the sins of the boardroom.

At no point during that season did I think that it might be my last at Liverpool. I always had confidence that we would be able to turn our fortunes around, that we might at least secure the fourth and final Champions League slot, and with it, the funds that would be crucial to the club's survival.

Indeed, I was so confident that, in December, I even offered a 'guarantee' to the supporters that we would finish fourth, an attempt to lift the club out of the dark mood which seemed to have settled on Anfield. I hoped that if I was positive, the fans and the players would be able to follow suit.

There were three teams competing with us for that position, with Aston Villa in contention, as well as Tottenham and Manchester City.

Right up until the start of May, we were in with a chance of retaining our place in Europe's elite competition, and it was only with Spurs' victory at City with two games to play that it was confirmed that we would not qualify, for the first time since 2004.

It was a huge disappointment, but a few days later we had the chance to rescue something from the season: the Europa League.

That competition had sustained us through the winter, as we contemplated our exit from the Champions League. True, it felt as though something was missing, as though there was an extra spark absent from those mid-week games under the floodlights, but that is unavoidable. For five years, we had taken on – and, more often than not, beaten – the best sides in Europe, in the best competition in the world. We had been to finals and semi-finals, tasted the greatest glory club football can offer. Now, we would have to make do with a pale imitation.

The chance to welcome some of the most famous clubs in football to Anfield should never be taken for granted, though. We had won the UEFA Cup – the Europa League's forerunner – when I was with Valencia, and there was no doubt in my mind that we should take it seriously. When you are in a competition, you try to win that competition. I do not know any other way.

Liverpool as a club, of course, is much the same, and the atmosphere at Anfield as we eliminated first Unirea Urziceni of Romania, then Lille and, in a wonderful display of attacking football in the quarter-finals, Benfica, suggested our fans were making the best of it, too.

Certainly, against the Portuguese team, dispatched 4–1 with two goals from Fernando Torres to dispel any lingering resentment for their victory over us in the Champions League in 2006, the noise and the passion on display were almost enough to match some of the famous Champions League nights we had experienced.

The semi-final pitched us against Atlético Madrid, a side we had met the season before in the group stages of the senior competition. Once again, Torres would not be fit to face his former club, after deciding to undergo an operation on the knee injury that had troubled him throughout the season, in a bid to make sure he was fit for Spain's World Cup campaign that summer.

And, as if our season had not been difficult enough, the presence of the Icelandic volcanic ash cloud which froze all air travel for a week or more meant that we would have to journey to Spain by train. Instead of a two-hour flight, we would require a two-day trip, travelling from Runcorn to London's Euston station, catching the Eurostar to Paris and spending the night in the French capital, before waking early and taking the TGV to Bordeaux, where we would either board another train, bound for Madrid, or, if travel restrictions had been lifted, a plane for the Spanish capital's Barajas Airport.

It was a long journey, setting off from Merseyside on the Tuesday morning, arriving in Paris that evening, before travelling to Montparnasse Station at around 7 a.m. the next day. In the buffet car of the train that was taking us to Bordeaux, I held an impromptu press conference, surrounded by a group of exhausted-looking journalists, cups and saucers rattling around me as we sped through southern France. Thankfully, once in Bordeaux, we could fly the final leg of the journey. Still, it was far from ideal preparation for a semi-final for the players, who were forced to sit down for hours and hours on a train, something which we normally try to avoid.

In those circumstances, our narrow defeat in the Vicente Calderón, to a very early goal from Atlético's Uruguayan striker Diego Forlán, was far from a poor result. We would have liked an away goal, of course, but that the Spanish team could not add to their lead offered us plenty of hope for the return leg at Anfield.

We were able to fly back from Madrid, an enormous relief. We did not want a repeat of the journey we had undertaken to get to Spain.

The return leg was the closest that season offered to one of Anfield's great nights. Our league form was still a cause for concern, and there were, by that stage, rumours about my own future and that of many of the players, but all of those disappointments and worries were put aside once we were on the pitch, under the bright lights, one step away from another European final. It was the sort of night where all that matters is the game.

Aquilani stroked us ahead just a minute or so before half-time to draw the scores level on aggregate, but we could not find a second goal. The clock started to tick. Both sides were tired. We would go into extra time.

When Yossi Benayoun, one of our best players that season, volleyed us ahead five minutes in, we were almost there, in Hamburg, ready to take on Roy Hodgson's Fulham for the Europa League.

Our season contained one more blow, though, one more mistake, one more slip that would bring everything crashing down. We failed to clear a simple long ball to the edge of our box. José Antonio Reyes picked up possession on the right-hand side, attacking the Kop, and swung a cross in. Forlán, formerly with Manchester United, met it, his fierce shot beating Pepe Reina. Atlético had an away goal. Atlético were going through. Atlético would go to the final. Our season was over.

At the end of April, Tom Hicks and George Gillett at long last agreed to put Liverpool up for sale, to end their involvement with the club altogether. They had been forced by the banks, as a condition of their latest loan, to appoint Martin Broughton, a Chelsea fan and the chairman of British Airways, to the same position at Anfield. Together with Christian Purslow, he would lead the search for new owners.

As the season drew to a close, I was informed on three occasions that I would have a meeting with Mr Broughton; all three, though, were scheduled far too close to games to be convenient, or even feasible.

When we did eventually meet, after the final game of our campaign, it was clear that we did not share the same vision for the future of the club. Broughton and Purslow asked me, in a series of conversations, how I saw the club moving forward, to which my response was that we had to stand by the plan that we'd always had: to build the academy, strengthen the side and, crucially, I wanted to be in sole charge of the team and of transfers, as I always had been at Liverpool. They did not give me any answer, any indication that such terms were acceptable to them, that they were prepared to start planning for the future.

It was at that point that it became evident what was about to happen. It was obvious that they had decided that my time at Anfield was up and wanted to come to an arrangement as quickly as possible. I was more relaxed, however. I was not in a hurry to leave Liverpool – quite the opposite: I wanted to stay. I told Purslow that I would go away on holiday with my family as planned, to Sardinia, for ten days, and that I looked forward to seeing him upon my return, when we would start to prepare for the next season. He was desperate, of course, to see the affair sewn up, to see everything put in order.

It was while I was in Italy that I next heard from the club. Their lawyers had contacted mine to offer me a settlement.

It was confirmation that the directors of the team I had worked so hard to turn into a force at home and abroad no longer wanted my services. I was disappointed, hurt and sad. I would not be given the chance to try to solve the problems that had arisen during the season, to complete the six years of work I had put into the club.

At that moment, it was clearer than ever that this was not the Liverpool I had joined, that I had grown to love; this Liverpool was a business, a franchise, and one that was not simply being run as a football club. Other factors were at play now.

I had four years remaining on the contract I had signed just a year previously, in the face of interest from another major club in Europe. I had decided to stay then because I had given my word to several players that I would not abandon them, that I would remain in place to try to win a league championship with Liverpool. Even then, though, the relationship with the owners was not the best: we differed on several key areas, but circumstances dictated that they needed me to be on a long-term contract, secured to the club, if they were to have any success in trying to sell up or to identify potential new investors. My continued presence had suggested a degree of stability and continuity, at least on the playing side. A year later, I was being told I was no longer required.

I mulled over the offer of a settlement. There was no use in fighting it. The club had evidently decided they wanted me to go, and in doing so, had offered me an insight into what Liverpool had become. We no longer had the same priorities, the same wishes. I told my lawyers to come to an agreement.

It was not about money, of course. I would not have held the club to ransom at a time when they had so many financial problems, thanks to the debts accumulated by the owners. I had no interest in personal gain.

I did, however, want to show my appreciation for all of the people we had met in the city during our time on Merseyside, and so, once an agreement with the club had been reached, I determined to make donations to a number of the charities that had become close to mine and Montse's hearts, including Hoylake Cottage and the Hillsborough Families Support Group.

On Thursday 3 June, the news was officially announced. I prepared a short statement for publication on the club's website.

'I'll always keep in my heart the good times I've had here, the strong and loyal support of the fans in the tough times and the love from Liverpool,' it read. 'I have no words to thank you enough for all these years and I am very proud to say that I was your manager. Thank you so much once more and always remember: You'll never walk alone.'

The club, too, had a statement ready. We had agreed to describe my departure as one made by mutual consent. 'Rafa will forever be part of Liverpool folklore after bringing home the Champions League following the epic final in Istanbul,' Martin Broughton was quoted as saying. 'But after a disappointing season, both parties felt a fresh start would be best for all concerned.'

That was, clearly, the club's view. I would have loved the chance to rebuild the squad, to restore the club to the Champions League places, but I would not be granted that privilege.

In six years, we had travelled across Europe, from the straits of Gibraltar to the banks of the Bosphorus, and we had won four trophies, including the one that guaranteed the European Cup would always reside on Merseyside.

In six years, we had beaten Real Madrid and Barcelona, Inter Milan, AC Milan, Benfica and Juventus, all of the great names of European football. We had run Manchester United close for the Premier League title, and we had added countless chapters to Anfield's already proud European history.

And now, six years after it all began, that adventure was at an end. Liverpool had changed beyond recognition. The days when Europe feared the thought of a trip to Anfield, when we swept all before us, were still fresh in the mind, but they already seemed impossibly distant. It was all over. I was no longer manager of Liverpool Football Club.

7

Season 2004–05
The Road to Istanbul

THE MOST IMPORTANT THING A MANAGER CAN HAVE IS trust. Players must have faith in their coach. They must believe you have the answer, whatever the question. They must have confidence, in the darkest moments, that you know the way.

It is a long process. It ended in the most remarkable of circumstances, at half-time in Istanbul, the players' heads bowed all around me, their worlds falling apart.

But it had started ten months previously, when I joined Liverpool from Valencia.

A Friday lunchtime, on a hot August day: we had just finished a light training session before preparing to travel to London for the first Premier League game since I had arrived in England, at

Tottenham. I called the squad together in the goalmouth of one of our pitches at Melwood.

'OK,' I said, in far from perfect English. 'We'll go from here to the other end at 80 per cent of our pace, and we will do it ten times.'

I pointed way into the distance, indicating that I wanted the players to sprint the full length of one pitch and then the width of another. They looked confused. It was an unreasonable thing to demand of them, less than twenty-four hours before a game.

Only Josemi, a player we had just signed from Málaga, dared speak. 'Ten times, hey?' he asked, in Spanish. 'It's too much.'

My reply was brief. 'You have to do it.'

And off they went. All of the squad, the day before a game, prepared to sprint a kilometre, maybe more, just because the manager said so.

'Come back, come back,' I shouted, before they had got too far. 'What are you doing?'

Exactly what I had told them to do, they said, now more confused than ever.

'You have to do what I say, of course, but you have to think too. I would like to hear more than just one person asking why I am making you do something, whatever it is. Sometimes, like now, I will tell you that it was just a test. And sometimes I will explain to you why I actually want you to do it. If you think, you will ask why. If you ask why I am making you do something, you will understand that I am thinking about this thing or that thing. And if you understand, you will trust me.'

That is, I suppose, my philosophy on management. Some

managers prefer to be more dictatorial in their style, to tell players what to do without an explanation. For some, that works. The players normally will do what they are told. For me, though, if possible, it is best to help them understand why they are being told to do something.

Understanding helps to foster a bond and, most importantly, it stops resentment. It means that if you explain a game plan, each person knows exactly what they are being tasked with. It means that if you rotate your squad, such a bone of contention in England, the players grasp what you are trying to do.

And it means that when all they have worked for seems lost, as in that dressing room in the Ataturk Stadium, they trust what you say. By that stage, they have learned that everything you do is for a reason. They know you have an idea. They know you have a plan.

This philosophy is not just for the training pitch. In those early team meetings, I would often set my players problems and challenge them to come up with solutions. I would ask a full-back how to deal with a certain situation, such as a winger dribbling the ball towards them. Do you let the ball come in, or do you close the player down? If you close him down, what do the centre-backs do? And the covering full-back? Every solution throws up another problem. What does the defensive midfielder do? Does he drop in between the centre-backs, or does he stand outside? You guide them to the solutions, but they have to understand the process, to realise why you play in a certain way or ask them to do particular things.

My way of doing things differed from that which Liverpool's players were used to, I think, but they responded to it fantastically well. Right from the very start, their attitude was incredible. They worked hard, trained well and were ready to consider new ideas. I was not surprised. After all, this was a squad prepared to sprint two pitches the day before a match at the manager's request.

They had the right approach, but I was less sure about their ability. I knew I was coming to a club in need of rebuilding. Rick Parry, the chief executive, had told me that when we first met to discuss the job. The squad needed an overhaul, he admitted, an infusion of fresh blood. I had played Liverpool with Valencia, in the Champions League and in a friendly, so we had all of our reports and notes. Together with my coaching staff – my assistant Pako Ayesterán, first-team coach Paco Herrera and goalkeeping coach José Manuel Ochotorena – I knew roughly what to expect.

The first training session, though, was still a bit of a shock. It is one thing to hear, and another thing entirely to see. Around a dozen of our senior players were still away on the first day of pre-season, granted extra leave after that summer's European Championships. Even so, what we saw at Melwood as we went through a gentle possession exercise was still a noticeable step down from the squad we had left behind in Spain, a team that included the likes of Pablo Aimar, Roberto Ayala, Rubén Baraja and a host of other internationals. It is easy to judge from the outside. Only once you see what it is like on the inside can you tell how much work there is to be done.

At least we had the return of most of our first team to look forward to. I had already been to see Liverpool's home-grown heartbeat – Steven Gerrard, Jamie Carragher and Michael Owen – while they were with England at Euro 2004, in Portugal. I had asked

Sammy Lee to request permission from Sven-Goran Eriksson, the England manager, to speak with them at their team hotel just outside Lisbon one day late in June, and he was happy to oblige.

I flew out, strangely, on the same plane as Steven's mother, Julie. I tried to ask her whether he wanted to leave, as was rumoured at the time, and to tell her about my plans for Liverpool, that I had come to win trophies and to make the team better, but my English at that stage was still a work in progress. She may have gone away with more questions than answers.

By the time I stood in front of Steven, Carra and Michael with a flipchart in a conference room in England's hotel, I was rather better prepared.

I explained how I saw each of them fitting into the side tactically, the way I worked, what my system would be, my vision for the team. We talked about what positions I felt would suit them best and I tried to show them that I knew how to get the best out of them, that I knew what I was trying to do.

I told them that we would be signing players, and they agreed that there was a dearth of quality in the squad.

'Training needs to be more intense,' they told me. 'We need players who have a winning mentality, who expect to be challenging for titles. And we need more depth, more players fighting for every position. People are relaxed if they aren't playing. We need competitive players on the bench, competition for places.'

It seemed to go well. They looked impressed at the detail of the presentation and appeared to be happy with my explanations and my ideas. They were excited at the prospect of change. Steven told me he would stay. It would prove to be a good decision. Michael, though, would not be persuaded to remain.

When I joined Liverpool, I knew there was some difficulty with Michael's contract. The club had been attempting to finalise a new deal before my arrival. That no agreement had been reached was telling, even to an outsider.

Michael told me as much when he and the other senior players returned from their extended break after the Euros. I called him into my office and asked if he was intending to go. He told me he was. From that point on, all I could do was try to get the best price possible for him. His contract would expire at the end of that season. We were not in a strong negotiating position.

It all came to a head the day of my first competitive game as Liverpool manager. We had returned from our pre-season tour of North America and, in the second week of August, were in Austria, preparing to play Grazer AK in the third qualifying round of the Champions League. It would prove to be the first step on the road to Istanbul. It was, though, the end of Michael's journey as a Liverpool player.

We met representatives of Real Madrid before the game. They told us they were interested in signing him, but that they were not in a hurry. They were prepared to wait until January, when they could sign an agreement to take him the following June for nothing. My contacts in Madrid, where I had worked for so long, confirmed they were not bluffing. I told Rick we had no choice: our position was weak, but we had to do the best for the club. We had to sell him right away.

It was imperative to keep the price as high as possible, so just a few hours after meeting Real, I named Michael as a substitute for our game in Graz. If he had played, the deal would have been dead: he would have been cup-tied for Europe, and Real would have walked away. If he had been omitted entirely, they would have known we were resigned to selling, and the price would have dropped.

Fortunately, we did not need Michael that night. Milan Baros and Djibril Cissé, signed by my predecessor, Gerard Houllier, played as strikers and Steven Gerrard scored twice to give us a 2–0 win, a good start as we tried to qualify for the group stage.

Four days later, Michael would be paraded around the Bernabéu as a Real Madrid player. We did all we could to get the best deal for Liverpool. We agreed an £8 million fee and I requested a young winger called Juanfran – now at Atlético Madrid – to be included as part of the deal.

He was a promising player, his quality obvious, but Real would not allow him to be released. I asked my friends at the club if there were any other wingers we should be considering, and they recommended Antonio Nuñez. He had played eleven times for Real the previous season, he had pace and they told us he was a good header of the ball. We included him in the deal.

Nuñez was really unlucky with us – he was injured in the first training session he had here, took three months to recover and then never showed the level we had been expecting – but fortunately our other signings that summer fared rather better.

We had bought Xabi Alonso from Real Sociedad, a young player of immense promise who had been rejected by Real Madrid for being 'too slow'. The fee we agreed to pay was heavily incentivised, meaning the more we won, the more Real Sociedad received. We fulfilled every single one of the criteria in Xabi's time at Anfield, I think, before he left for Madrid five years later.

I had known Luis García since my days at Tenerife. I had taken him on loan from Barcelona, and he had something a little bit different about him: game intelligence, a special talent, vision that was not quite the same as that of the average player. He could play in three or four positions and, though he would have poor games, he would also have matches where he was unstoppable. We knew he had a release clause at Barcelona of just £6 million. Like Xabi, Luis wanted to come, and he wanted to win.

Our final signing found life a little harder. Josemi's partner had just had a child and he found it hard to learn the language and to settle into life in England. We wanted a hard defender, good in the air, strong in the tackle, but the Premier League maybe did not suit him.

I, too, had plenty to get used to. There is a lot to learn when you start in a new league, even as a manager. The referees, in particular, are different: it surprised me constantly, in that first year, what was deemed a good challenge, particularly in the air. For me, my assistants and the Spanish players, every single one was a foul.

The benches, too, were different. I remember my first game at Anfield, against Kevin Keegan's Manchester City. We won the match 2–1, but because the opposition dugout is right next to the home one, whenever Kevin stood up to shout an instruction to his team, I could not see the game; likewise, whenever I went into the technical area, his view was blocked. The benches were so close that I had to start issuing orders in Spanish, calling one of the Spanish speakers across so that he could pass the message on. Otherwise, the other team hears what you are doing, and counteracts it immediately. I had never had to deal with these things in Spain.

Settling in away from the pitch was a little easier. We had found a home on the Wirral, and Montse was enthusiastically learning about the culture and history of the city, then passing on what she had found out to me in the evenings, telling me things she felt I needed to know.

I was supposed to be learning English, too, but after two lessons it became clear that I did not have time to fit my classes in. We were moving too slowly, and I needed to learn so that I could talk with my players immediately. I told my teacher, recommended to me by the club, that it would be better if I taught myself, by reading the newspapers, listening to the Beatles and watching the television with subtitles on, so I could learn the words more quickly.

There was so much else to do that it was impossible to concentrate properly on anything but football. I was always at Melwood. Depending on traffic, I would be in my office by 8.30 a.m. every morning, and I was often not leaving until seven or eight in the evening. They were long days, trying to arrange deals, talking about players, conducting training, mapping out schedules and watching forthcoming opposition. There was so much to learn.

We knew we had to get our ideas across to the team quickly. We had held an introductory meeting, soon after our arrival, with the entire squad, going through the same things I had told Steven, Carra and Michael that day in Portugal. We explained how we saw the team developing, what we wanted to do, how each of the players fitted into our plans.

But it is not simply a matter of talking to the players once and then getting on with work. To establish trust, to build that relationship, you have to maintain a constant dialogue. I held individual meetings with each of the senior players, to see what they wanted to improve, what they felt needed to change if the club was to be successful again. I called in Sami Hyypia, Dietmar Hamann, Steven and Carra, as well as all the new signings. And we spoke in less formal settings too: in my office, on the stairs, on the training pitch, in the canteen. Every time we had an opportunity, we would discuss things with the players, find out how they felt, how they thought we were progressing. By the time of the second leg against Graz, when we confirmed – despite a 1–0 defeat – our place in the Champions League group stage, we had held countless conversations, making sure everyone knew where we were going, and how we were planning on getting there.

Everyone was jumping, pouring off the bench in disbelief. In front of the Kop, the players were leaping for joy, piling onto Steven Gerrard. There are certain things only players like him can do. The fans were bouncing around, hugging, dancing. The noise was deafening, the atmosphere electric. As I turned to the bench, a steward, clad in orange, gripped me and gave me an enormous cuddle. I was not jumping. All I was thinking was that we had four minutes still to play, and we needed to do things properly.

People often remark that I do not show any emotion, do not look like I am enjoying myself when a goal is scored. It is not that at all;

quite the opposite. I am always proud and, on nights like that, you can feel how much it means to everyone. It sends a shockwave through you.

It is just that you have a chance to pass a message on in those few seconds. During a game, it is hard to communicate things to your players, particularly those on the other side of the pitch. They cannot hear you and, obviously, you cannot call people across. When a goal is scored, I try to find someone in the middle of the park, someone who can spread my word. That night, I wanted them to know they had to keep calm. They had just four minutes to hold on.

We seemed to exist on the edge that season, and here was a prime example. We had come within a whisker of being eliminated from the Champions League at the group stage, waking up the next morning as a team in the Europa League. Nobody at the club wanted that. If we could survive for four minutes, we would avoid that fate.

It had been a difficult group campaign. The draw in Monte Carlo at the end of August had paired us with Monaco, finalists the previous season, Deportivo La Coruña from Spain, a fine side that I knew well, and Olympiakos, the Greek champions and a mainstay of the competition. Though Liverpool were, of course, a famous name across the continent, I don't think any of our rivals were particularly intimidated at the prospect of facing us. We had a new manager, new players and we had not even been in the competition the previous season. We were not an established force. Not yet.

We made a good start, beating a Monaco side that included Maicon, Patrice Evra and Emmanuel Adebayor 2–0 at Anfield, thanks to Djibril Cissé and Milan Baros, but we lost our second game, away at Olympiakos. Their fans are so noisy, so passionate. It was a hard evening for our players. The home side scored with a header from a free kick, through Ieroklis Stoltidis, and though Harry Kewell thought he had equalised for us in the second half, it was ruled out for offside.

Our next game brought Deportivo La Coruña to Anfield. That was a fine side, who had enjoyed a lot of success in the Champions League in recent seasons. They had Juan Carlos Valerón, a wonderful player, as well as the experience of Fran, Mauro Silva and Víctor, a winger who we would later try to bring to Liverpool. It was no surprise that they held us to a goalless draw at Anfield, leaving us with four points from our first three games.

The trip to La Coruña, in November, was a chance for Montse to return to Galicia, the region of Spain in which she grew up. It is very famous for its seafood, and the night before our game, as we all settled down for dinner with the players, she told us that we had to taste the local speciality: *pulpo a la gallega*. Octopus, boiled with paprika, salt and olive oil. A delicacy. It was absolutely wonderful, and the Spanish contingent – Ocho, Pako Ayesterán and Paco Herrera among the coaches, and players Luis, Josemi and Xabi – sounded their appreciation. Some of the other members of the squad seemed to disagree: Carra and John Arne Riise, a Norwegian, particularly, looked thoroughly disgusted. I don't think they were particularly impressed with Galician cuisine.

It did not affect their performance the following evening. Riazor is a very English stadium, with the steep stands towering over the pitch and the wind howling in from the ocean, and we produced an excellent performance.

We knew from the first leg how hard we would have to work to stop Deportivo. We needed to be very compact, because their movement was so intelligent and their forwards, Albert Luque, Walter Pandiani and Diego Tristán, were so dangerous. Valerón and Fran moved between the lines, switching positions, trying to prise the defence apart with penetrating passes. We stuck to our task.

We were without both Steven and Xabi Alonso, ruled out at the very last minute with a calf injury, and we had to draft Igor Biscan in to a reshaped midfield. He played with great energy and desire.

It was not spectacular, but we were dogged and determined. Milan Baros, a lone forward, forced Jorge Andrade into an own goal after fourteen minutes, and we might have scored more. It was the best I had seen Liverpool play since I arrived.

That victory put us joint top of the group, along with our next opponents, Monaco. Qualification was far from assured, though. We could not afford a slip.

The Stade Louis II, Monaco's home ground, is not an enjoyable place to play. It is only a very small stadium, with a capacity of just 15,000, and because there is a car park below the pitch, the surface is very hard, very bumpy.

It is even less enjoyable when, inside four minutes, one of your players – Luis Garciá – is stretchered off, injured. We would lose Josemi, his replacement, later on in the game too, after he clashed heads with Evra, leaving our Spanish defender needing several stitches to staunch the bleeding.

By that stage, we were already a goal down – to a strike from

Javier Saviola — and our hopes of securing Champions League qualification there and then were beginning to fade away. This was made all the more galling by a clear handball from the Argentine striker immediately before he shot past Chris Kirkland, something the Danish referee, Claus Bo Larsen, told my players he had seen. It was an incomprehensible decision, and one that left us needing to beat Olympiakos by two clear goals at Anfield if we were to remain in the competition and avoid the ignominy of seeing our campaign ended before Christmas.

To me, that game against Olympiakos was the very first great European night I experienced at Liverpool. I knew all about the passion of the fans, the atmosphere they could create, but that is something you have to witness first hand, rather than just hear about. I am not sure why it should be, but the Champions League always seemed to bring out the best in our supporters. It was Anfield at its most powerful.

The stadium is different at night. The sound changes, the noise is more raw, running down the Kop and pulsing through the ground. It takes your breath away. Maybe it is because the fans have had to wait all day for the game. Maybe it is because on a weekday — and particularly in the knockout rounds, when there is so little time between the draw and the day of the game — the crowd tends to be more local. To me, the crowds on European nights always seemed more Liverpudlian. That year, perhaps it was simply the excitement of seeing Liverpool involved, once more, in the competition that has always meant so much to the club's supporters.

In the dressing room, as the atmosphere outside was building and the tension mounting, the noise seeping through the walls, we were trying to remain calm. We knew what we had to do.

Half-time. A goal down, to one mistake, a hole in our wall, allowing Rivaldo to curl a low free kick beyond Chris Kirkland and into the Kop net. We needed three, in just forty-five minutes. The ideas we discussed then would become familiar that season.

'We just need a goal and then we'll see what happens,' I told the players, as they sat, spirits low, in the dressing room. 'We need to relax. If we get anxious, we will lose control of the game. Calm down, and play with pace, but do not hurry. We have time.'

I moved on to explaining the tactical changes. There was space outside the box, so we had to look for our striker – Milan Baros – and then try to win the second balls. We had to play with more width, get the ball into wide areas and be careful not to cede possession too easily. Olympiakos were looking to play on the counter-attack and, with Rivaldo's vision and talent, they would be dangerous. I wanted to cross the ball early, to test their defence, and for both full-backs to stay high.

Most of all, though, I wanted us to keep calm.

There are times when keeping a cool head is the most crucial ability a player can possess. It was the same three years later, when I removed Steven in the second half of a finely poised Merseyside derby, bringing on Lucas Leiva. Only with a calm mind can you find the right pass, make the right decision. Emotion clouds your judgment. Against Everton, as against Olympiakos, we could not afford for that to happen.

Against the Greeks, I would also make a substitution. Florent Sinama-Pongolle had great pace, tremendous confidence and the ability to beat players. He would replace Djimi Traore. We instructed him to play between the lines, get out wide, take his opponents on. We wanted his energy and his dynamism.

'If we get an early goal, we can do this,' I said, as the team strode out. 'Keep calm. Think.'

The impact was immediate. Sinama-Pongolle darted into the six-yard box fifty seconds later to meet Harry Kewell's low cross, tapping it home with his left foot. Kewell missed another two chances. Gerrard had an effort ruled out for a foul. The pressure built. Olympiakos did all they could to hold on, but they were moving backwards. Rivaldo's goal, maybe, had tricked them into thinking the game was over. We swarmed forward. They could not control the game. But we could not find a second goal, and we still needed two more. The clock ticked.

We decided to bring on Neil Mellor, a young player but a natural finisher, to replace Milan Baros, who had worked so hard.

It took two minutes this time: Sinama-Pongolle crossed with his left foot and Antonio Nuñez, another substitute, headed towards goal. Antonis Nikopolidis palmed it away, but Mellor reacted quickest, stabbing the ball home. There were nine minutes left.

When I had first taken the Liverpool job, Rick had told me that I would be given three years to reshape the team, three full seasons before I would be expected to challenge for the Premier League title, to start delivering trophies. That has never been my attitude, though. I wanted to win every competition we entered in that first year, even the Champions League. I certainly did not want to see us knocked out at such an early stage.

Carra picked up the ball on the left wing. Now the fans were roaring us on. The clock showed eighty-six minutes had passed. This was the famous Anfield atmosphere, back once more after all these years, the stadium that all of Europe once dreaded. Carra looked up, picking out Mellor. The striker cushioned a header back to Gerrard, waiting in all that space on the edge of the box that Olympiakos had left unguarded. We know what he can do in moments like that: a perfect connection, a half-volley, from twenty-five yards, screaming beyond Nikopolidis, into the net. The entire ground was jumping. And I was being given a bear-hug by a steward.

We held on, as the stands swayed and sang. After the game I made sure to shake hands with every single one of the players, and all of the coaches too. This was a moment that belonged to everyone. We would be in the last sixteen of the Champions League. We were still in the competition the fans longed to be part of, and that I – probably uniquely – genuinely believed we could win.

All four of us shuffled into the cramped, busy pub. Together with Pako Ayesterán and 'Ocho' Ochotorena, Alex Miller, our first-team coach, and I had been sitting in the team hotel in Cologne wondering how we would be able to watch Chelsea play Barcelona in the second leg of their Champions League round-of-sixteen tie. Our hotel did not have the channel which was showing the game on German television.

'There's an Irish bar in town,' suggested Alex. 'They have Sky. We'll be able to watch it there.'

The hotel found us a taxi and off the four of us went, talking about our game the following evening with Bayer Leverkusen. We were leading 3–1 from the first leg at Anfield, but there was still much to prepare.

It was only a short journey, perhaps a few minutes, before we pulled up outside the bar. I paid the taxi driver and we walked inside. We could not go far, because there were so many people, all wearing red Liverpool shirts or with red and white scarves draped round their shoulders, standing in front of the bar, craning their necks to see the screen.

We stood and watched what was happening at Stamford Bridge. Alex was on my right-hand side, with Pako to my left and Ocho just behind. We had not expected so many people, but we were happy simply to watch the game, quietly, and then slip away. That was the plan, anyway.

As we were watching, another man, just to the side, glanced across at me. He looked away. Then he glanced back at me again. 'Rafa!' he shouted. 'Rafa's here!'

'Ssshhhh,' I said, raising my finger to my lips, worried that the entire pub would hear, desperate to quieten him down so that we could keep on watching the game.

It did not work. Suddenly, every single person had turned around from the big screen and was staring at us. And then a huge roar went up: 'Rafa's here, Rafa's here.' People started streaming forward, shaking my hand, congratulating us. A woman started kissing my cheek. We tried to tell them, 'OK, OK, watch the game, watch the game.' It was impossible. We knew we had to leave, but there were fans all around us now. We couldn't move. We edged forward, shaking hands, smiling, saying hello to everyone we could, slowly, slowly inching towards the door. It can only have been a few metres between us and outside, but it took maybe ten or fifteen minutes to get there. And then, when we reached the safety of the door, we walked out and there were two absolutely enormous fans outside, two huge Scousers, shaking our hands, hugging us.

Soon the pictures would be posted on the internet. It was an incredible experience: I knew about Liverpool's fans, of course, but I had never met so many all at once. It had never occurred to any of us that we might not be able to stay in a bar, even one full of supporters. All we had wanted to do was watch the game.

After all, we knew we might play one of those two sides, José Mourinho's Chelsea or Frank Rijkaard's Barcelona, at a later stage in the competition. Our first-leg victory at Anfield over a strong Leverkusen team that included Carsten Ramelow and Bernd Schneider, both World Cup finalists with Germany in 2002, as well as Dimitar Berbatov and Andriy Voronin – a player we would sign two years later – had left us well placed to qualify for the quarter-finals.

That we had managed to win that first leg without Steven Gerrard or Xabi Alonso was even more impressive. We had known, because Berbatov's touch was so good, that we had to win the second balls if our central defenders, Carra and Hyypia, could not control him. Leverkusen's system relied heavily on their wide players, so we had instructed our midfield to come narrow when we did not have possession, and we knew we needed to be aware of Ramelow's bursts from midfield too. They liked to pass the ball out from defence, so we told Luis Garciá and Milan Baros, our forwards, to press them as high as they could.

In that first leg at Anfield, we had scored early, through Luis, before Riise added a second with a free kick. By half-time, we were in a strong position. 'Don't rush anything,' I had told the players at half-time. 'Play the goal kicks long. Try to stretch them, and make sure we don't give Berbatov too much space.'

When Dietmar Hamann scored our third late on, our place in the quarter-finals had seemed as secure as you could hope for. Like I say, though, that season we seemed to exist on the edge. We switched off for just a second in injury time and Franca, Leverkusen's Brazilian striker, scored a consolation to keep the tie alive. We would have to be more careful in Germany.

Sometimes I think that trip to Leverkusen, for the second leg, is remembered only for the night in the pub in Cologne, but in truth that was one of our best away performances in Europe. We had killed the game off by half-time, thanks to two more goals from Luis, and when Baros scored a third in the second half, it was obvious the fans who had made the trip were really pleased. More pleased, perhaps, than they had been the previous night to see their club's manager in the bar!

We managed that game very well. Leverkusen's threat came largely from set pieces, so we had adapted our marking strategy a little, going more man-for-man than we ordinarily liked to. That flexibility is something I had tried to teach the players from the very first day: the zonal-marking system was criticised in England, but most teams are more flexible. More often than not, for any individual game, your defensive strategy at set pieces is something of a mix. When we played Chelsea in the Premier League that season, for example, we detailed Salif Diao to man-mark John Terry, who had scored a number of goals from corners that season, while the rest of the team were set up to mark zonally. It was the same in Germany. Some man-to-man marking, some zonal. You have to adapt to the circumstances of the individual game.

The problem with a lead in the first leg, of course, is complacency. It is crucial, particularly in a competition like the Champions League, where the standard is so high and the opponents so dangerous, that a team retains its focus until the very last kick. This is where rotation, another concept so roundly scorned in England, can be very useful. By drafting in players who are competing for their place, a manager can ensure his team has the intensity needed to win these games. It can keep everyone in the team on their toes.

Our aims for that evening were simple: we had to keep the tempo high, try to engineer one-on-one situations for Luis and, most of all, we needed to retain possession. 'Move the ball,' I told the players as we prepared for the game. 'Look for Steven from the goal kicks, win the second balls and then keep possession. That is the main thing. Play it simple.' That is the best way, the only way, to take the sting out of a game, to deprive your opponents of hope.

By half-time, it was obvious that Leverkusen – who needed to score six goals in the second half to qualify – were beaten, but we urged the players to keep their tempo up, to continue playing simple, not to give them so much as an inch. Our hosts could only muster a late consolation goal. We would be in the quarter-finals.

In later years, seeing our name in the draw for the last eight would become a regular occurrence – only once would we be absent between then and 2010 – but I think it is probably fair to say that most of the teams left in the competition wanted to face us. They saw us as lesser opponents than many of Europe's richer clubs. Our league form was patchy. We had been humiliatingly dumped out of the FA Cup by Championship side Burnley.

Xabi Alonso had suffered a broken ankle in a challenge with Frank Lampard during a 1–0 defeat to Chelsea on New Year's Day, and Fernando Morientes, the striker we signed from Real Madrid that January, was cup-tied. Steven Gerrard had endured injury problems of his own. We were something of a patchwork team. Nobody at the club had even dared to suggest we might reach the final, let alone win the tournament. Compared to the likes of Chelsea, AC Milan and Bayern Munich, I suspect most of our rivals saw Liverpool as a gentle draw.

There was only one team remaining who did not want to face us, and even they would have been confident of beating us on the pitch. Juventus, I suspect, did not want to play Liverpool because of what the game would mean away from it.

For once, the mood at Anfield was downbeat, almost sombre, as we walked out onto the pitch to the strains of 'Zadok the Priest'. That was no surprise. That night in March 2005 was the first time Liverpool and Juventus had met in the twenty years since thirty-nine fans of the Italian club lost their lives at the Heysel Stadium in Brussels before the 1985 European Cup final.

We had hosted a game at our academy, in Kirkby, between groups of Liverpool supporters and some of the travelling Juventus fans, to try to build bridges between the two clubs. Before we kicked off that night, there was a highly emotional presentation on the pitch, with the Kop unveiling a banner which read: 'Friendship'. Some Juventus fans turned their backs on the gesture. A minute's silence, respectfully observed, followed. The atmosphere was one of sadness. The stadium felt tense.

In truth, managers and players remain a little remote from such things: it is our job, on both sides, simply to prepare for a hugely important game. I am sure, though, that my counterpart Fabio Capello, like me, knew the significance of the occasion. In the dressing room, though, we did not know what was happening above us.

In the hour and a half after we arrive at the stadium but before kick-off, there is so much to do: the players can go out on the grass, to check the surface, before coming back inside. I name the team, explain the tactics, and then those who want massages are given them, before we go out for the warm-up. I try to be around the dressing room throughout. Some managers disappear, but I like to speak to individual players about their roles in the game, perhaps offering them a bit of advice or support.

That night, we had much to distract us from the poignancy of the occasion. With Jerzy Dudek not fully fit, Scott Carson, at nineteen, would make his Champions League debut. It was the biggest game of his life. Xabi, still recovering from that injury suffered on 1 January, was only fit enough to make the bench. Dietmar Hamann could not play at all. We would have to draft in Anthony Le

Tallec to play as a forward, alongside Milan Baros.

Signed by Houllier as a teenager, there was no question that Anthony had plenty of talent. He was a very gifted player, but still very raw, which meant we simply could not afford to play him in his preferred role, behind a central striker. As a forward, it was a little bit different: he could win the ball in the air, hold it up, bring others into play. Nevertheless, it was his first appearance in the competition. Our resources had been stretched to breaking point.

This, after all, was hardly the time to be playing experimental teams lacking in experience. Our opponents were one of the most accomplished teams in the world, with Alessandro Del Piero and Zlatan Ibrahimovic up front, the Italian international captain Fabio Cannavaro in the centre of defence and Pavel Nedved, the Czech international, playing in a free role.

Although by that stage Nedved was reaching the end of his career, he was one of our primary concerns that evening: his long-range shooting was of the utmost quality and we knew we would be in trouble if we allowed him space to gather in second balls.

Nedved was central to Capello's 4–3–1–2. I had come to know Fabio quite well early in my career, spending three days with him while he was manager of AC Milan, watching his training sessions at Milanello, learning all I could from one of the most successful managers of the modern era. He had a team befitting his status, and one full of confidence. Juventus had beaten Real Madrid in the previous round and were no doubt sure they would see off the rather less impressive challenge of Liverpool.

We would have to be alert to stop them. Steve Finnan would

have to move inside to watch Nedved, while it would take two defenders to deal with Ibrahimovic, one challenging him for the ball and the other screening in front of him.

Our attack, on the other hand, would rest on Milan Baros's running, as it did so often that season. His task was to try to dart in behind the defenders, leaving Le Tallec to drop deep, pick up possession and try to seek him out. That was the only way we could play. Looking at the line-ups, few people would have thought we stood a chance.

Ten minutes in, that didn't matter. Baros's persistence won a corner. Gerrard swung the ball in, and Luis, running to the near post, flicked it on. Sami Hyypia, in the centre, peeled off his marker, ran to the back of the six-yard box and met the ball, sweeping in a volley at the Anfield Road End. It was a movement we had worked on in training in the run-up to the game.

Suddenly, where the fans had initially felt weighed down by the maudlin occasion, they were uplifted. The noise was even louder than usual, the fans singing my name – to the tune of 'La Bamba' – and 'Ring of Fire', the song they had adopted as their anthem for that campaign.

Fifteen minutes later, they almost lifted the roof off the stadium. Anthony Le Tallec, dropping deep, flicked a pass over Baros's head. The ball bounced perfectly for Luis, twenty-five yards out, to send a dipping shot over Gianluigi Buffon and in. Anfield exploded. Again, I did not react, because there was so much still to be done. We had to keep calm, to keep doing the right things. A manager has to stay focused. I cannot let myself be swept up in the emotions.

At half-time, I tried to be business-like, to concentrate the players' minds. Juventus were a side of tremendous quality. Their attack relied on a lot of penetrating passes from midfield. We had to be careful. 'Don't try to anticipate the pass,' I told Sami Hyypia, who had, on one or two occasions, almost been caught out trying to get in front of Ibrahimovic. 'Don't try to step in front of him. Stand off. And keep an eye on his lateral movement. Don't go too far with him, don't let him drag you out of shape.'

They were trying a lot of short corners, something we needed to be aware of if we were to keep Juventus at bay. As for us, as always that season, we just had to keep running. They were playing very narrow, with the full-backs moving forward to provide their diamond midfield with some width. We would have plenty of success exploiting the space they left behind, so long as we kept switching play quickly.

By the end of the game, though, we would not feel nearly so positive. One slip, in the Champions League, can be so costly. Scott had done so well on his European debut, but then he allowed a header from Cannavaro to slither through his grasp and into the left-hand corner of the goal.

Suddenly, the tide had turned. Juventus had an away goal. Once more, a repeat of their result against Real Madrid a few weeks previously would be enough to see Capello's team into the semi-finals. Once more, we stood on the edge.

13 April 2005: Juventus 0–0 Liverpool

Juventus: Buffon; Thuram, Montero (Pessotto, 83), Cannavaro, Zambrotta; Camoranesi (Appiah, 84), Emerson, Olivera (Zalayeta, 46); Nedved; Ibrahimovic, Del Piero
Liverpool: Dudek; Carragher, Hyypia, Traore; Finnan, Nuñez (Smicer, 58), Alonso, Biscan, Riise; Luis Garciá (Le Tallec, 85); Baros (Cissé, 75)

At the centre of it all was Xabi Alonso. He had not played since 1 January, spending three arduous months recovering from his broken ankle. We knew, though, that we would need him in Turin. With Steven Gerrard ruled out with a thigh strain, he would be the cornerstone of our team that night.

We had targeted this game for his return as soon as we had progressed against Leverkusen in the previous round. He had slowly, steadily, stepped up his recuperation, spending time in Spain with specialist physiotherapists before returning to England and to Melwood, first jogging in training and then resuming work with the ball. But without ninety minutes at a full, competitive level, he would still be short of match fitness, more fragile than we would like. We would require a system to protect him.

Rather than play in our usual 4–2–3–1 formation, I decided to switch to three central defenders – Carra, Hyypia and Traore – with Steve Finnan and Riise deployed as wing-backs. In the middle, Xabi would play deep, with Igor Biscan and Antonio Nuñez acting almost as bodyguards, doing the running that he simply was not fit enough to do. After just a week or so of intensive training, there was no way

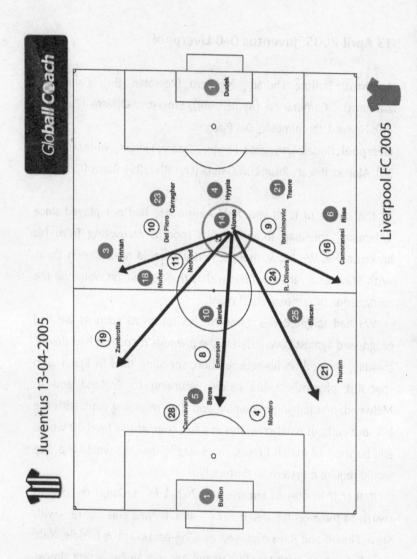

Xabi Alonso was at the centre of everything. His lack of fitness as he recovered from an ankle injury meant we would play Biscan and Nuñez as his bodyguards, and task him simply with picking out the runs of Baros, Luis Garcia and the others.

he would have been able to maintain a full tempo for ninety minutes. He needed to hold his position, not run too much. There would be others to do that for him. Their job was to feed him the ball; his was to play long, picking out the runs of Milan Baros, our lone striker. With our resources so depleted by injury, there was little else we could do. That season was one of making do with what we had.

Necessity, as they say, is the mother of invention. Such a system had the added benefit that it might offer us more control of their two strikers, Del Piero and Ibrahimovic, with five defensive players and Xabi in front of them. The 4–3–1–2 formation so favoured by Italian teams encourages them to play through the centre, rather than utilising wide areas. In Gianluca Zambrotta, Juventus had one of the best full-backs in the world, but even with him overlapping, they would still come down the middle. If we could flood the midfield and be first to the second balls, play compact and narrow, we could shut down their attacking threat.

It was imperative, too, that we did not sit too deep. Even on nights like that, when keeping a clean sheet to protect your 2–1 aggregate lead is all you need to do to ensure qualification, I would never encourage my team to sit back, to drop right to the edge of our box. If you play deep, you will make a mistake. My idea is always, always to push out, to get the ball as far from our goal as possible.

We worked on that new system in the days leading up to the game, taking special care to make sure Xabi knew his role for the evening. The atmosphere was just as tense in Turin as it had been in Liverpool for the first leg. Our fans had been cooped up all day in a medieval castle, to prevent them spilling onto the streets; in the stands and around the crumbling Stadio Delle Alpi, Juventus supporters were fighting with each other and with the police.

In the dressing room, we went over the detail of our approach. Play long for Baros. Luis would try to make the most of the space created in his wake, looking to pick up on second balls. Keep the line at what we call 'three-quarters' – not too deep, not too high – and be aware of their attempts to play off Ibrahimovic. 'Don't allow their midfielders to run beyond you,' I told the five players who would play in our midfield. 'Play simple, keep possession as much as you can, and when we switch the ball, press immediately, as high up the field as you can. Xabi, be ready to hit Baros.'

That was our idea. We had one more trick up our sleeves.

Instead of instructing the team to line up in our specially designed formation, I told them to play for the first two minutes in the 4–2–3–1 that Fabio Capello and the rest of Juventus's coaching staff would probably have been expecting. Only after the game was underway would we move, organically, into the 3–5–1–1.

It is a little trick that managers sometimes use. Often, if your opponents see you start the game in a different way from the one they had anticipated, they will react, adapting their own system to counteract yours. That is the manager's job, of course, to change his approach depending on circumstances. If you change after a few minutes, it can look more natural. Sometimes, your rivals will not alter a thing.

And so, that night, we moved into our new formation after a few minutes. Juventus remained in their 4–3–1–2, playing through the middle, their illustrious forwards kept largely quiet by our three

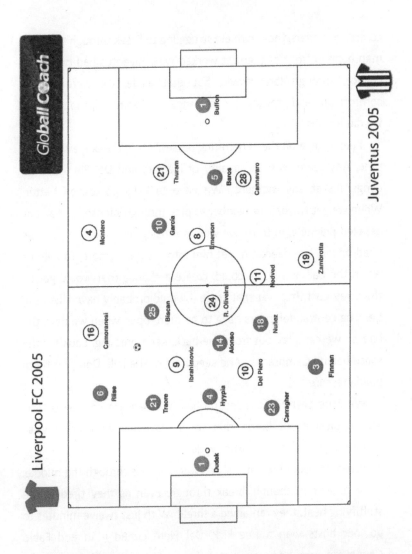

Our system changed organically in the opening few minutes as we tried to outfox Juventus a little, moving from the 4-2-3-1 Fabio Capello had probably been expecting into a 3-5-1-1 which allowed us to protect Xabi Alonso a little more, as well as deal with their high-quality strikers.

central defenders, their midfield struggling to break through the five-man bank in front of them. It worked well: Juventus had one early chance, through Ibrahimovic, but that aside, we were largely comfortable, and growing in confidence. It was crucial, though, that we did not lose focus.

'Keep an eye on the penetrating passes,' I told the players at half-time. Any team with the quality of Nedved and Del Piero can be dangerous at any moment. 'We have to keep possession better. When we get the ball, remember to play through Alonso.' For all our detailed planning, in truth, we were not using him quite as much as I had hoped. We needed to get him into the game more, to help us retain the ball and, if we could, create a chance that would get us the away goal that – at that stage – would probably have killed the tie. 'The central defenders have to be more open when we have the ball, so we can play out from the back. Keep pressing. Look for the space behind Camoranesi. And keep hold of the ball. Don't let them build pressure.'

We were better in the second half. We had one counter-attack, Alonso picking out Baros, that might have earned us that goal, allowed us to breathe. He shot wide.

Juventus poured relentlessly forward, always through the middle. They could not, though, break through. Even as they tired in the stultifying heat, they remained a threat. With just twelve minutes to go, our hosts won a free kick. Del Piero curled it in and Fabio Cannavaro, who had scored at Anfield, leapt to head it against the post. Traore cleared it from the line as Juventus protested that a goal should be given. Their appeals were waved away.

We were tiring, too, after all the energy and effort we had invested in holding out. We needed fresh legs. I put Le Tallec and Cissé on to try to stretch Juventus's defence, to occupy their thoughts. Cissé's pace, particularly, would be the last thing our hosts would want to contemplate after seventy-five minutes in the warm, oppressive air of northern Italy, as they were desperately trying to find a way past, resorting more and more to the long ball. Capello's side were hoping for a lucky bounce, for one last mistake, right at the death. It would not come.

As the players celebrated their victory, congratulated each other on their determination, their doggedness and their spirit, their triumph of will, it would have been unfair to seek them out and explain to them where they might have done a little better; the strikers' movement, for example, was not as good as it should have been. Sometimes, I do like to speak to the players on the pitch, certain ones, those who are most receptive to new ideas: Xabi and Carra, in particular, were always ready to improve, to learn something different.

It may seem a strange time to point out little tweaks to their game, but it is best to speak to them when things are fresh in their minds. On the plane, they like to sleep, and after a lot of games you do not see them for one or maybe two days. You must strike when you can, to drive the message home.

Not that night, though. That was a time for the players to enjoy. This team – without their captain, without Dietmar Hamann, one of their most experienced players, and with a central midfielder who was far from fully fit – had reached the final four of the world's biggest club competition. This was no time for lessons or advice, even though our thoughts were already turning to the semi-finals, and to the familiar foes who waited there.

We had already faced Chelsea three times that season: at Stamford Bridge and at Anfield in the league, and in Cardiff, at the Millennium Stadium, in the Carling Cup final. All three had been close games, the two matches in the league decided by single strikes from Joe Cole and the League Cup final won by Chelsea in extra time. We had been leading, thanks to a goal from Riise, until Steven scored an own goal in the seventy-ninth minute.

That season, there was little indication of the rivalry that would soon arise between the two clubs, certainly not between the two managers. I had never encountered José Mourinho before that first year in England – our paths had not crossed – but we had enjoyed a perfectly cordial relationship.

At Anfield on New Year's Day, we had bumped into each other on the stairs leading to the boardroom. Despite the events of the game – when a tackle from Frank Lampard had broken Alonso's ankle, and Cole had scored late on to deprive us of a well-deserved victory – we stopped to talk, a polite conversation about our respective work and the ambitious plans of Chelsea's owner, Roman Abramovich, for that summer's transfer market. It was a brief chat, but a reasonably friendly one. He even said in his press conference before the game that if we overcame his side over two legs, he would be happy to see us go on and win the Champions League. 'We have a good relationship,' he told the media under the strip-lights of the press room at Stamford Bridge.

It would not last.

Mourinho deserves credit, though, because his Chelsea side were one of the best I have ever faced, in the same class as Barcelona or Real Madrid at their best. They could hurt their opponents in countless ways.

They had players capable of cutting a defence apart with a penetrating pass. They could play on the counter-attack, at great pace, with incredibly quick wingers like Damien Duff and Arjen Robben. They were a threat from set pieces – John Terry, as I have said, had scored a lot of goals that season from corners and free kicks, and we knew we would have to take special measures to deal with him – and they could build the attacks from Didier Drogba, hitting the Ivorian with a long pass and then playing off second balls.

They had so many options, so many ways of causing damage, as all of the top sides do. They scored so many goals, of so many different types. That season, their pursuit of the Premier League title was relentless. They had already won the Carling Cup – albeit narrowly, requiring extra time to overcome us in the final – and it was only a matter of time before they lifted the league championship cup, too.

Liverpool, on the other hand, were in a period of transition. We knew we would have to be perfectly prepared if we were going to stop them. But we had shown, against Leverkusen and Juventus, that while we were still far from complete in the league, we did not need to fear anyone over two legs. In these types of matches, it is easier to close the gap. 'If you look at the games we have played, there is not much between us,' I told the press the evening before the match.

It was true. We had been close to them every time we had met. But still, nobody in that room at Stamford Bridge expected us to be the English team in the final. This, everyone thought, would be the end of our road.

The only way we could make up for the difference in quality was to focus. We named a line-up whose emphasis was very much on solidity: Alonso and Igor Biscan would sit deep in midfield, with Steven Gerrard slightly further forward, and Luis Garciá and Riise playing wide. Once more, Baros would have to run into the channels, trying to create space between the lines.

We set our defensive line, as we had in Turin, at three-quarters. Not too high, not too deep. We could not afford to invite Chelsea to attack us: a team with that many attacking options would score, for certain, if we tried to defend the edge of our box. And we practised the offside trap, too, because Mourinho's team looked to Tiago, the Portuguese midfielder, to play penetrating passes behind the defence.

Our team talk – the previous day and in the hour before the game – concentrated on all the things we would have to do just to keep Chelsea at bay. 'Close the passes, make sure they cannot counter-attack, and watch for the switch of play,' I said. We altered our marking on set pieces slightly, too, to make sure we had Terry covered man-to-man, not simply by the zonal system. We talked about how to counter-attack, of course – rapid switches of play, making sure we made the most of our set pieces – but we knew it would be an evening for resilience, rather than beauty.

The players stuck to their task well. Chelsea had a lot of pressure that evening, but not so many good opportunities to score. Milan

Baros might even have given us a precious away goal in the first half, but saw his header saved by Petr Cech. We would have the advantage for the second leg, but it would be a slender one. Even then, the game ended on a sour note: Xabi Alonso was booked, in the last few minutes, for a foul on Eidur Gudjohnsen. Xabi was furious. He felt he had not touched the striker at all. The appeal was useless. He would miss the second leg at Anfield through suspension.

In a drawn game, that was a small but significant victory for Chelsea. Mourinho's team had such quality, such organisation, that facing them with your strongest side was a daunting prospect. Seeing one of our best players suspended, so unfortunately, was a considerable blow to our hopes.

For all their disappointment, Chelsea's position was hardly weak. They travelled to Anfield knowing that scoring just once – as they had in the league – would force us to score twice if we were to travel to Istanbul. They remained favourites to reach the final. At Anfield, though, at night, things are always different.

3 May 2005: Liverpool 1–0 Chelsea

Liverpool: Dudek; Finnan, Carragher, Hyypia, Traore; Luis Garciá (Nuñez, 84), Biscan, Hamann (Kewell, 72), Riise; Gerrard; Baros (Cissé, 59)
Chelsea: Cech; Geremi (Huth, 76), Ricardo Carvalho, Terry, Gallas; Tiago (Kezman, 68), Makelele, Lampard; Cole (Robben, 68), Drogba, Gudjohnsen

Already, the noise was creeping through the walls. Outside, anticipation was mounting. Nervous, excited, frenzied, anxious. Long before the sun had set, it was obvious this would be a night nobody would ever forget. Liverpool were within ninety minutes of returning to the European Cup final.

The fans were pouring into the ground, carrying banners and flags, singing songs that expressed their hopes and dreams. They greeted us as our coach drove through the Paisley Gates, past the Hillsborough Memorial and to the entrance of the Main Stand. A huge roar, to make your hair stand on end, went up as we descended the stairs of the bus. Before the team escaped down the white-washed tunnel of the players' entrance to the safety and serenity of the dressing room, they had just a taste of the spine-tingling sense of destiny, the crackle of excitement, coursing through the city.

It is at these moments that a manager must be an island in the maelstrom.

So often, the message you transmit to your players must be the opposite of that which they are feeling, of what the fans are thinking. If they are nervous, you must be confident. If they are too confident, if they feel we are due to play a weaker side, we often tailor our team talk to highlight the opposition's strengths. When we play opponents better than us, we show our squad the chinks in their armour, the points at which they are most vulnerable.

If you sense that the players are a little flat, that they do not realise the importance of the occasion, then you must try to inject some passion into them, to rouse them from their torpor with a stirring speech, perhaps. And, as was the case as they completed their final preparations before facing Chelsea, ninety minutes from Istanbul, from the Champions League final, from history, if you sense they are nervous, you can only try to exude an air of calm. It would not help to push them too much, to highlight the importance of the occasion, when there is already so much at stake.

On these occasions, it is your job to manage anxiety, to remind them how well-prepared they are, how much work they have done, to calm their nerves a little. Much of that is done through establishing a routine: players will react badly if things are done differently from normal, or at all haphazardly. You must create an environment where they know exactly what is to happen during the day in the build-up to a game, so that they can pour all of their energy into their jobs, so that they are not distracted in the slightest.

That begins the night before, gathering the squad together at a hotel, so that they all sleep well, without distractions. The next morning, we all have breakfast together, hold a final team meeting, eat a little lunch – some pasta for the players, as ever – before resting in the afternoon. It is the same before every evening game. That is the key: everything should be familiar. Then, when the players board the bus at 4.30 p.m. to drive, under police escort, to Anfield, they are completely focused and as relaxed as it is possible to be an hour and a half before one of the biggest games of any player's career.

Once ensconced in the dressing room, I let the players walk out onto the pitch, should they wish to, to see the surface for themselves, remind themselves of their surroundings. Even if they have played there hundreds of times before, they often like to spend a few minutes on the pitch, talking to their team-mates. When they return

– and not before – I will name the team. Routine. Everything always the same.

'Dudek, Finnan, Carra, Hyypia, Traore, Luis, Hamann, Gerrard, Biscan, Riise, Baros,' I said, before naming our seven substitutes. We would have John Welsh, Stephen Warnock and Carson on our bench, along with Cissé, Nuñez, Smicer and Kewell. Chelsea's, with Mateja Kezman, Robben and Glen Johnson, was worth millions. It highlighted the chasm between the two teams.

I am not nervous at those times, regardless of the game. People often ask if I am ever overwhelmed at the scale of the task in hand, thinking about all of the fans filling up the stadium, each one of them hungry for victory. When you are so focused, though, so absolutely concentrated on the task in hand, you cannot think about anything else. I know how hard we have worked, how well we have trained. I know that we have prepared everything perfectly, poring over DVD footage, practising set-piece routines, analysing the opponents, passing our knowledge on to the players. Each game is simply the culmination of a process lasting days, based on research dating back years, decades. I know we are in control. My job is to transmit that to the players, to tell them what the plan is. To show them that you have a plan.

'We have nothing to lose tonight,' I told them, trying to make sure they were not paralysed with apprehension. 'Chelsea are the favourites. Everyone is talking about them. Whatever happens, we stick to the game plan. The tactics remain the same. We do what we have to do, we carry on, and we stay focused. Don't lose concentration, not even for a second. That's all.

'Don't sit too deep. Push out as soon as you can. We need to stay compact, really tight, to fight for each other and to support each other. We know they will try to play a lot of penetrating passes, looking for Drogba, so be aware, close them down. Be careful in our half. They are dangerous from set pieces, so no fouls. Don't give them the chance to get the ball into the box. We clear the ball long, we get it away, and then we fight for the second ball.

'We keep possession and we play it simple, as simple as we can. We need our midfield to support Baros, to get forward into space. Luis and Riise, you have space to go forward. And if we score, if they score, we just keep on doing the same things.'

It was the sort of occasion where your experienced players have to come to the fore.

Dietmar Hamann had played in a World Cup final with Germany and won two Bundesliga titles while with Bayern Munich. In the absence of Alonso – suspended for that yellow card late in the first leg – he would be key. We needed Kaiser to keep possession, to switch play, looking for spaces behind Chelsea's full-backs, to give sense and definition to our game. Beside him, Gerrard, so often our driving force, would have to move to one side or the other to create space and to receive the ball. That was how we intended to build our attacks.

I always try to be around the dressing room, after naming the side, running through the tactics and explaining set pieces on the flipchart, as the players listen to music, talk, or simply sit, quietly, to focus themselves for the game. That season, Cissé and Luis Garciá tended to be in charge of the music in the dressing room, but many

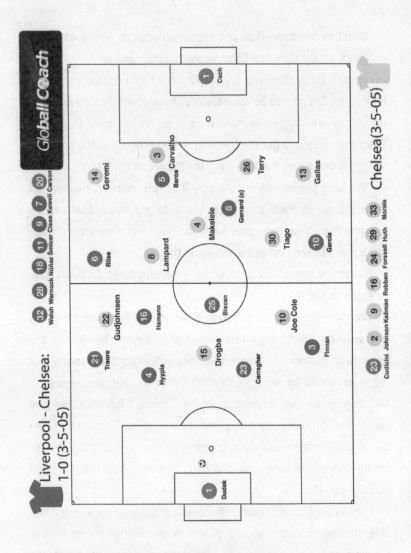

That Chelsea team was one of the strongest I have faced, and we knew a player of Dietmar Hamann's experience would be crucial on such an occasion. He would screen our defence, with Steven Gerrard tasked with roaming between the lines and creating the space we would need to build our attacks.

of their team-mates would have their own headphones on. A few would ask specific questions about members of the opposition, what they should expect, and we tried to put their minds at rest. That night, though, we all knew what was coming: the Premier League champions, a team built at a cost of millions, crowned the previous weekend at Bolton.

We walked out into a storm, a tempest. They told me later that Anfield set a record for noise created at a football match that evening. It was not a surprise to learn that. I think, though, that the sound stunned Chelsea. I am not sure they expected to meet such a wall of noise. It startled them. By the time they had recovered their composure, we led.

It was a goal, of that I am certain. My secretary, Sheila, told me as much after the game. She had been sitting in the section for club employees, roughly level with the goal-line at the Kop end. It crossed the line, she said. I have no reason to doubt her. She was always incredibly reliable.

More importantly, what was so often forgotten about Luis Garciá's goal – the ghost goal, as Mourinho named it – was that, had it been disallowed, we would have been given a penalty and seen Petr Cech, Chelsea's goalkeeper, awarded a red card just four minutes into the game. In many ways, I think Chelsea got off lightly.

It was a move that deserved a goal. Riise played the ball in to Gerrard, who flicked a pass into Baros's path with his first touch. Baros clipped a shot over Cech and was brought down by the goalkeeper. Luis followed up and touched the ball over the line. And, according to Sheila, despite William Gallas's attempts to clear the effort, it went in. Anfield agreed. The ground erupted in delight, fans spilling over seats, hugging each other. Istanbul was so close, a return to the grandest stage in European football was almost tangible.

My mind, as ever, was on the remaining eighty-six minutes. I had to make sure the players did not lose their concentration, did not allow their focus to slip.

I did not need to worry. Anfield rocked, the ground shaking as songs and chants washed down the Kop and crashed over the rest of the stadium, and we stood our ground. Chelsea, the mighty Chelsea, could manage just a few attempts on goal in that first half. Dudek barely had a save to make. We made it to the dressing room unscathed.

'We have to keep working,' I told the players. I had pulled Carra aside to warn him to keep his arms down when challenging Drogba, something that is largely accepted in the Premier League but will be penalised every single time by a referee in Europe. We could not afford to give Chelsea a golden opportunity to draw level from a set piece. 'Get close to Drogba,' I said to the rest of the team. 'They will play long to him, hitting him quickly from the back, and then look to regain the ball. We have to stay compact. Stick to the game plan. Be close, challenge him, and then be ready for the second ball.'

That is how Chelsea approached that second half: long balls up to their powerful striker, and then hoping to play off him. Such a method is a little bit of a lottery, not particularly scientific, maybe a little crude. There was no subtlety to their play.

The pressure was growing. We needed fresh legs. Baros made way for Cissé, who was ordered to stretch their defence, to occupy their thoughts, to ensure that they could not throw everything forward. His pace would cause them problems. We were winning, but we could not afford to rest. We had to try to get behind their back-line.

Still the onslaught which we expected did not come. Mourinho brought on Robben, but there was no change in style. Long ball, second ball. Long ball, second ball.

It almost paid off. Chelsea almost won the lottery in the last six minutes of injury time. Robben had made a couple of chances, but how frustrated Mourinho was became clear when Robert Huth was sent on to play as a striker. Another high ball came into the box, with less than sixty seconds separating us from Istanbul. Dudek came to punch, but his contact was not good enough. The ball fell to Gudjohnsen.

The clock seemed to stop, to miss a beat. Everything hung on that shot.

Gudjohnsen cocked his right leg and volleyed the ball, a perfectly controlled effort across goal. The noise abated. Everyone held their breath.

It fizzed wide. Chelsea sank to their knees. Anfield exhaled, in relief, in joy, in sheer, unbridled delight. Our players raised their arms in triumph and their eyes to the heavens. It was not, in truth, until I saw the video after the game that I realised how close it had been, how narrowly Gudjohnsen had missed. History turns on such fine margins. Liverpool, not Chelsea, would be in the Champions League final. Only AC Milan stood between us and history.

* * *

There was still much to do that night. The celebrations on the pitch lasted for ten minutes, maybe, congratulating the players, embracing the staff and consoling Chelsea's team. There would, of course, be no cordial talk with Mourinho that evening. Our 'good' relationship was over. He had now identified us as a threat, as a team who could stop him achieving all that he wanted. There would be no more courtesy between Anfield and Stamford Bridge.

Instead, I went straight from the dressing room, the sound of the anthem still ringing in my ears, to the trophy room, where we hold our Champions League press conferences. It is full of reminders of Liverpool's illustrious history, trinkets and pennants earned from European games going back forty years or more. We now had our chance to add to that history.

The round of interviews lasted for half an hour, maybe more, speaking to television, radio and newspaper journalists from across Europe. Even on a night as special as that, my approach to press conferences is normally the same: it is important to respect your opponents, praise your players and express your pride at what you have done. If something out of the ordinary happens, then usually you should comment on it, though not always. That night, one reporter asked me if I had seen the ball cross the line for Garciá's goal. I preferred not to say anything. Not until I had spoken to Sheila.

By the time I returned, the players and the staff had decided to hold an impromptu party. I wasn't particularly keen, seeing as we had only reached the final, not yet won the tournament, but my coaches, the players and – most importantly – Montse were of a rather different mindset. 'You'll be in the European Cup final,' said my wife. 'We're having a party.'

There was no room for debate. It is not that I do not enjoy those moments – far from it. I know how hard we have all worked – players and staff – but it is not my style to be extroverted, to have a public celebration. I prefer to relax with a few friends, surrounded by the people I work with, to assess what we have done, and how we have done it. I suppose I am a naturally analytical person.

On that occasion, though, I was outvoted. The whole city was celebrating – or at least the parts of it that supported Liverpool – and nobody at the club wanted to miss out.

Someone arranged to book the Panam, a bar on the Albert Dock on Liverpool's waterfront, situated inside the Britannia Pavilion, a beautiful, listed building with exposed brick ceilings and high, vaulted archways. Players, friends, family, coaches, staff: everyone travelled from the ground to be there and to toast our achievement.

It was a wonderful atmosphere. I was taught the words to a lot of the songs that we had heard on the Kop that season: 'Ring of Fire', the Johnny Cash song that had been adopted as the anthem of that European campaign, and the chant the Kop had made for Luis Garciá, which had rung out so loudly after he had scored that night. The party lasted until the early hours of the morning, with everyone drinking champagne, talking, relaxing, celebrating all that we had achieved.

That was the first night that I was introduced to Robbie Fowler, who had come, along with Steve McManaman, to join his friends and congratulate them on reaching Istanbul. He is a special person,

Robbie. We had only just been introduced when he started encouraging me to sign him. It did not happen immediately, but he had something to offer the club, and his love for Liverpool was obvious. He would return soon enough.

By the time the party moved on to the Sir Thomas Hotel in the city centre, I had departed for home. My mind that night was not on commemorating how far we had come, but was considering how far we had to go. As the players and the staff were attempting to get lifts home, I was already considering AC Milan and PSV Eindhoven, the two teams in the other semi-final: how we would beat them, how we could stop their strikers, and what we would need to do if we were to become European Champions again, for the first time since 1984.

People who were at that party that night have told me that I was the only person still talking about football, at least when I was not being taught how to sing some of the Kop's favourite songs. That certainly sounds like me. There was nothing to celebrate yet, as far as I was concerned. A manager can never waste the chance to prepare for a forthcoming opponent, can never afford to rest when he might be learning. I was trying to discuss the strengths of Milan and PSV with my coaches.

As soon as the next morning, the players would be coming to me with questions. It was crucial that I should have answers. I had to show them that we had a plan to beat whoever we would face in Istanbul, on 25 May. One that would make us champions of Europe. One that would restore Liverpool to its former glory. One that would give the club its pride back.

8

Heroes

'IF THAT ONE COMES FIRST, WE WILL LOSE,' I SAID.

I had been enjoying a quiet dinner with a few of my coaching staff in our hotel on the outskirts of Istanbul. Now we were waiting to go back to our rooms, the night before the Champions League final. A bank of four lifts was in front of us. I pointed from left to right.

'If that one comes first, we will win. If it's that one, we draw, and lose on penalties. If it's that one, we draw and we win on penalties.'

We waited.

With a high-pitched ping, the fourth lift, on the far right, sounded its arrival. We would win on penalties.

I am not, in truth, a superstitious person.

I can only remember having two lucky charms in my career. Throughout that season, I used a Mont Blanc pen to make notes during European games. It became something of a talisman. It also accompanied us on the journey to Cardiff, and the FA Cup final, the following year. I was so attached to it that when, on the return journey, I was told I could not take it in my hand luggage, I refused to board the plane back from Wales to Liverpool. We negotiated for an eternity before it was agreed that the captain would take the pen, and reunite me with it upon touching down at John Lennon Airport.

I also wore the same pair of underpants for every European game in my first year at Liverpool. They had been selected for me by my daughter, Claudia. She would plead with me to wear them every time we had a Champions League game. There are times when you simply cannot argue with a six-year-old girl. Unfortunately, the item in question was bright red and bore the face of the Tasmanian Devil, the cartoon character. She had chosen them while I was still working for Valencia and I had worn them while winning La Liga and the UEFA Cup. She insisted I wore them for every European game. Resistance was futile.

The pen is still at my family home, in West Kirby. The underpants have been repaired, and are awaiting fresh challenges.

Instead of superstitions, I prefer to concentrate on hard work, perfect preparation and not leaving anything to chance. Especially in Istanbul: the biggest game of my life and of my players' careers. After two decades in the wilderness, Liverpool could stand proud among Europe's elite clubs. After two decades, Liverpool were back in the European Cup final.

We arrived three days before the game, on the Monday morning. We wanted to give the players plenty of time to relax, to settle in to their surroundings, to get used to the heat. If you stay at home, you are pestered by people wishing you luck, wanting to see you, asking for tickets. It is far better to whisk them all away to a secluded hotel, away from all such distractions, where they can prepare in peace.

You can use the time wisely: light training sessions, a visit to the stadium to get used to the surface and the height of the floodlights – for goalkeepers, that is particularly important – so that, on the day of the game, nothing disrupts your rhythm.

The worst thing you can do, as a manager, is allow the players to grow bored, leaving them with nothing to do but lie on their beds and watch the clock. Before games of such importance, a football club develops a curious atmosphere: players are excited, but they are nervous too, and determined not to show it. You have to keep them occupied to keep them focused.

On that first day, we held a team meeting. The idea was to give the players confidence for the game, to show them that we had a plan to beat a Milan team widely recognised as the best in Europe. My English at that stage was not sufficiently good to prepare the meeting in anything other than Spanish. At times, it can be hard to convey emotion in a second language, or to speak with the same finesse. I felt it went well, though.

'Milan are the favourites,' I told the players, once they had assembled in one of the hotel's meeting rooms. 'But we are hungrier. We want to win titles. Maybe we want to win titles more than they do. If we want it to happen, if we really believe it can happen, then we will win.'

I tried to highlight that everyone in that room deserved to play in that game, that nobody was surplus to requirements. After all, everyone had done their bit to help us reach the club's first final since 1985. Florent Sinama-Pongolle and Neil Mellor, for example, had both scored against Olympiakos, ensuring that our campaign was not over at the group stage. Even youth-team products like Stephen Warnock and Darren Potter had played their part.

'Everyone has a chance to play,' I said. 'You have all been involved on the way here. All of you have a chance, and even if you don't start, one of you may come off the bench and score a decisive goal.' Vladimir Smicer, of course, would prove that to be the case.

We talked about a lot of things. What we would do if we were winning at a certain point, what we would do if we were losing. How to react if we had problems, if things did not go to plan.

'We must play as a team, just like we did against Chelsea in the semi-final and Juventus in the quarter-final. We need effort, intensity, belief from every single one of you. Most of all, we need confidence.'

That is crucial: players must not fear the consequences of losing, so much as long for the rewards of victory. We knew that, because we had only finished fifth in the Premier League, we had to win on Wednesday night if we were to have any hope of returning to the competition at all the following season. I did not want the players to have that at the back of their minds. The pressure was great enough.

'If you win this game, it will go on your CV. It will be there forever. You will go down in history. It is not very important if we are in the Champions League next year, if you are not here next season. But if we win, we will always have this.'

* * *

I slept in a little that morning. Normally, at home, I wake up at around 5.30 a.m. or 6 a.m., have some cornflakes and milk and go straight to my office to analyse the previous night's game, draw up training schedules or watch forthcoming opposition. When I am in a hotel, I allow myself a little extra rest.

The day before, Tuesday, we had made the long journey to the Ataturk Stadium for a light training session. It is not a particularly stringent test for the players, more a chance to make sure they know what to expect and to run through certain specific aspects of play with particular individuals. The majority just do some exercises, get a touch of the ball, and then depart. There is no point in staying too long. It is better for them to be relaxing in the hotel, perhaps watching DVDs of their opponents, focusing on the task in hand.

I am the same. On Wednesday morning, I wandered down to have a light breakfast – eggs, a little cheese and ham, maybe a yoghurt – with my coaching staff, going through a few details of our tactical plan. The mood was light. The players knew the scale of the task awaiting them, but also the exciting opportunity they had.

Our team talk that morning, between breakfast and lunch, was designed to reinforce all the things that had taken us to Istanbul. We wanted to press our opponents, high up the pitch, from the very first whistle. It did not matter whether we were losing or winning, I told them, we had to play the same way we had against Chelsea, against Juventus, against Olympiakos. We had to play with our hearts.

Then, the technical side: one central midfielder would have to sit and hold, another would have to move forward. It was the same for the full-backs: if one goes, the other stays. We needed to look to

Xabi Alonso and Steven Gerrard to switch play behind Milan's attacking full-backs. We ran through the various signals for our set pieces.

And we needed to be aware of the dangers Carlo Ancelotti's team, complete with Andriy Shevchenko and Kaka and Hernán Crespo, posed. Our analysis team had prepared clips to illustrate their approach to set pieces. Milan would try to pack the box with bodies for corners and free kicks. We would have to watch for that.

Lunch is always a simple affair. The players tend to eat pasta or rice, something relatively plain, because you cannot force them to eat something they genuinely don't like just to fill their bodies with carbohydrates. I ate with them, rice and eggs, before we rested for the afternoon.

It seems strange that, just four or five hours before a game watched by millions of fans all around the world, players – and coaches and managers – are able to sleep, but it is crucial. The players must have as much energy as possible – and the manager, too, I suppose. It would be a late night. I would need to be well-rested.

I never have trouble sleeping before games. That afternoon, I went to my room with an armful of DVDs of Milan's games from that season. Our analysis department at Liverpool were excellent, watching a host of fixtures and noting regular moves, preferred styles of play, set-piece routines, but as much as I trust them implicitly, I also trust my own judgment. By watching a game in its entirety – rather than just the pre-prepared clips – I might see something they have missed, or interpret something in a different way. The analysis team know exactly what I want to see, but sometimes I want to see everything with my own eyes. With just a couple of hours to go before we would have to board the coach, I settled down on my bed to see what Liverpool were in for that night.

All through that day my phone would beep every few minutes with another message wishing me and the team good luck. They came from Merseyside, of course, but also from across the world and, in particular, from Spain. It is the manager's job to stay calm even when everyone around you is bristling with anticipation. You have to remain composed. You have to be ready.

It was nearly 5 p.m. when we left for the ground. We could see from the coach the distance the fans would have to travel to the stadium, even after arriving in Istanbul. We could see how bad the traffic was as supporters began to descend on the Ataturk. The effort and commitment they were making was incredible.

Timing is everything before a game. It is key that you do not get to a game too late for the players to prepare properly, but also important that they are not at the stadium for too long with nothing to do. That allows their nerves to build. Players are creatures of habit, I suppose. They are at their best when they have a set routine that is followed wherever they are and whatever the circumstances. That allows them to concentrate solely on performing at their best.

We got to the stadium with perhaps an hour and a half to go before kick-off. Perfect. They would have a chance to go out onto the pitch, get a feel for the surface, and return to the dressing room to be told what the team would be. Some would react with excitement and delight when it was confirmed they would be starting in the biggest club game on the planet, the most important fixture they would ever play. Others would be distraught when their names were not read out, when they were told they would begin the biggest night of their lives on the bench.

There are two sides to preparing any game: the defensive and the offensive. A manager must consider both not in isolation, but as parts of the same whole.

Against Milan, much of our defensive preparation centred on Kaka. We knew all about the dangers he posed, of course, how lethal his surges through the centre could be, and we knew that in Shevchenko and Crespo, Milan had two of the best strikers in the world for him to supply. As a trio, they functioned superbly well together. Without Hamann patrolling in front of the back four, we would have to look to Xabi Alonso and Steven Gerrard to control Kaka. We would need to be compact and, crucially, we would need to be first to the second balls.

In attack, our idea was to use the quality we had. It would be impossible to stop their counter-attacks if we did not have the ball. Alonso and Gerrard offered us the best chance of doing that, with Kewell playing between the lines. We knew we would need to be in control of possession to have any chance of victory, and we felt that playing the Australian just behind Milan Baros – rather than Hamann as a third central midfielder – would enable us to do that.

Baros's movement relentlessly dragged defences out of shape. Kewell would be able to dictate play and orchestrate our attacks in the space he created. His responsibilities, though, did not end there: he would have a second job too.

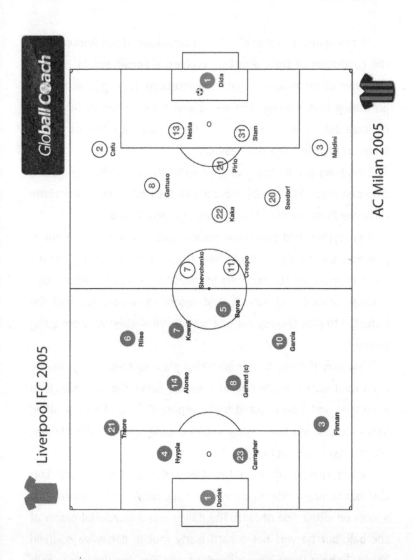

Our original idea was to prevent Milan's counter attacks by depriving them of the ball: Harry Kewell started, playing behind Milan Baros, to enable us to retain possession between the lines. Xabi Alonso and Steven Gerrard would be tasked with controlling Kaka's forward bursts.

At the centre of Milan's 4–3–1–2 formation stood Andrea Pirlo, the conductor of their attacking orchestra. Kewell would have to close him down as soon as we lost possession, staying close to him, pressuring him, staying alert for second balls, so the Italian international did not have the time, or the opportunity, to look for his forwards breaking past our defence.

Like Juventus in that season's quarter-finals, Milan played a diamond shape in midfield, leaving it to their full-backs, particularly Cafú, the Brazilian World Cup winner, to provide width.

That system had two consequences. First, when we were not in possession, our wingers would have to come inside, playing narrow so as to make up the numbers in midfield, to prevent Milan overloading Gerrard and Alonso. And second, it meant we had the potential to play two against one in wide areas when we were going forward.

That was the key to our attacking plan: to switch play quickly from midfield to isolate one of their full-backs. On one side, John Arne Riise and Traore would try to expose Cafú, and on the other, Steve Finnan and Luis Garciá would double up on Paolo Maldini, Milan's legendary captain.

In the middle of the pitch, Harry Kewell, Gerrard and Luis Garciá, roaming inside from the right wing, would look to exploit the spaces on either side of Pirlo. The Italian was a wonderful passer of the ball, but he was not a particularly mobile defensive midfield shield. To have those players breaking past him into the box as balls came in from wide areas represented, we thought, our best chance of success.

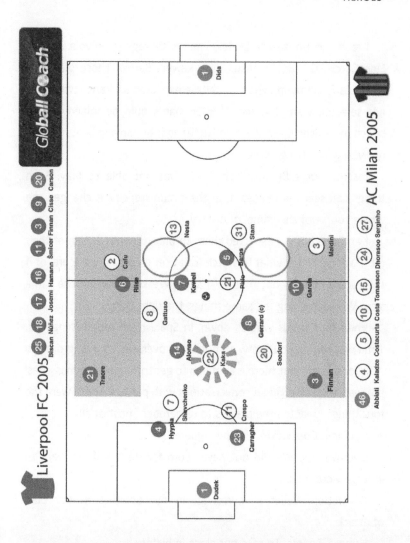

Our attacking plan centred on Kewell and Gerrard making use of the space either side of Andrea Pirlo, Milan's deep-lying midfielder, who was not the quickest when playing as a defensive shield. We also wanted to double up on the wings – Traore and Riise on the left, Finnan and Luis Garcia on the right. Kaka, though, was finding too much space behind Alonso and Gerrard.

I read out the team. 'Dudek, Finnan, Carragher, Hyypia, Traore, Luis Garciá, Gerrard, Alonso, Riise, Kewell, Baros.' Those players – particularly Hamann, who would have expected to start – who were not selected were deflated. The German would be joined on the bench by Smicer, Cissé, Antonio Nuñez, Igor Biscan and Scott Carson, our young reserve goalkeeper.

Josemi, our substitute right-back, was not able to play. Such things can seem insignificant. In the circumstances, it changed the whole course of the game, of history.

I explained how I expected them to play, described each of their jobs, went through what to watch for at set pieces. 'If we score, or if they score, it does not matter,' I said. 'We keep playing the same way. We keep doing the same things, the right things.'

I had four words written down, in Spanish, to round things off. Time was running out now. An hour, just over, seems a long time to wait for a game, but there is so much to get through – the massages, the warm-ups, individual conversations with players. These were the four things I wanted the players to remember, most of all.

Decision. Convicción. Hambre. Quererla.

Decisiveness. We did not have room for doubts if we were to emerge victorious.

Conviction. Belief in ourselves, in our abilities, in our plan of attack.

Hunger. To win. To take our place in history.

Want the ball. Do not hide under the lights, under the pressure. Stand together with your team-mates. Want to win.

* * *

'Make sure the first pass goes long,' I said, after the players had returned from the warm-up and were making their final preparations. The noise in the dressing room was starting to rise, some offering shouts of encouragement to release their tension, some going through their final, personal rituals. 'Look for Baros running.'

I wanted to make sure we were on the front foot from the very start of the game, that we were not inviting pressure, allowing any nerves to get the better of us. It was important that we showed straightaway that we intended to attack Milan. The first pass shows your intention. I wanted the ball near their goal, not ours. I wanted the first pass to be a statement of intent.

The first pass did not go long. The first pass went short. It was misplaced. Milan won a free kick. They packed the box with bodies. Pirlo swept the ball in. Maldini, with his right foot, twelve yards out, drove it past Jerzy Dudek. We were a goal down barely a minute in.

That is the fate of the football manager: we had worked for weeks to prepare the game, to make sure the players knew exactly what to expect. When they walked from the dressing room to the tunnel, as they waited there, side by side with their opponents, some exchanging greetings, some staring straight ahead, immersed in their own thoughts, the mounting roar from the stands filling their ears and inspiring their minds, I was confident they were ready. We had done all we could to perfect everything, to the very last detail. We had controlled all we could, right until that very first pass.

By the bench, I could tell that most of the stadium was red. I could see the banners fluttering among our supporters, hear the familiar songs. My focus is always completely and utterly on the game, so I am only partly aware of the atmosphere. Everything extraneous to the match has been shut out.

Slowly but surely, our game plan was falling apart. Kewell signalled to the bench that he had to leave the pitch, injured. Smicer, in his last game for the club, was sent on in his place.

Milan scored again. One moment, we should have had a penalty, Alessandro Nesta handling the ball as he lay sprawled on the ground in his own box. The next, Kaka broke forward, bursting ahead of Gerrard and Alonso, feeding Shevchenko on the right-hand side. The Ukrainian's low cross gave Crespo a simple tap-in.

That was when I knew we had to change the system. With that lucky Mont Blanc pen, I scribbled a note to switch to three at the back. I knew that Hamann would have to come on, and that he and Alonso would have to take a less offensive position, to sit deeper, to staunch Kaka's breaks through the middle.

We would have three against two at the back and then two midfielders, controlling space. In possession, two of our central defenders would fan out wide, to allow us to build attacks through Alonso. With Riise and Smicer hugging the touchline, we would have five attacking options. Through the middle, Gerrard and Luis García would have to try to maximise the space either side of Pirlo, and Baros would stay high, to force Milan, who were still in the 4–3–1–2 in which they had started the game, back. That was how we would claw back our two-goal deficit, how we could get back into the final.

Six minutes later, on the cusp of half-time, just a few seconds from the sanctuary of the dressing room, where we could change

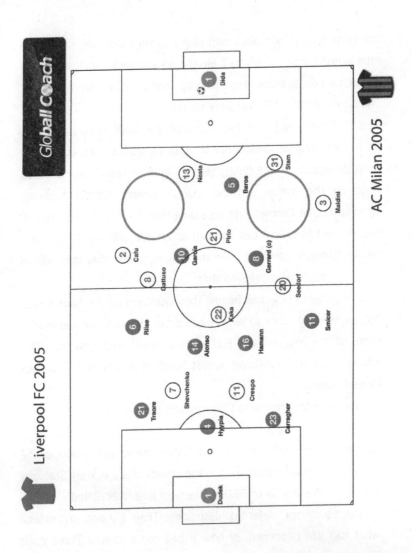

The introduction of Dietmar Hamann at half-time helped control Kaka: Hamann and Alonso sat deep and we switched to three at the back, using wing backs, so that Garcia and Gerrard could attack the areas Pirlo did not cover.

our system, alter our plans and begin to turn the tide, Kaka span Alonso just inside Milan's half. He slid a sixty-yard pass just beyond Carragher's outstretched leg and in to Crespo, on loan from Chelsea. The Argentine lifted it over Jerzy Dudek.

3–0. I could tell that the sound of the stadium had changed. Milan were jubilant, their bench in raptures, their players ecstatic.

In the stands, in the family section, Montse was crying. She was watching the match with her aunt, Carmen. Montse told me afterwards that Carmen kept repeating that it was not over, that all was not yet lost. 'We can still win it, we can still win it,' she was saying. Carmen may have been the only person in that stadium, on or off the pitch, who believed that.

Our players hung their heads. They crouched on the floor, heartbroken. We had come so far. We had done so much. We had beaten some of the best sides in Europe to be here. And now this. This embarrassment. It was over almost before it had begun. They sank to their knees.

These are the moments that measure you as a manager.

All around me, heads were bowed. Players stared at the floor of the sweltering dressing room, deep in the bowels of the Ataturk Stadium. The noise, the crackle of 50,000 Liverpool fans, was dulled.

The squad sat, dejected, despairing. They did not understand what had just happened, or how it had come to this. Three goals down in the biggest game of their lives, unable to comprehend where and why it had all gone wrong.

This is where the journey we had started back in July, at the very start of pre-season training, the very first day that I met my new players in my position as Liverpool manager, drew to a close.

There are two sides to management. One is the coaching of players as footballers, improving their fitness and their technique, teaching them to adapt to your tactics. The other is to convince them that, no matter what happens, no matter how dire the situation, you have an answer. It is making them believe that you have a plan. Every training session you take, every game you play, you must reinforce that message.

This is why I had encouraged them not simply to follow my instructions, but to question them, so that I might explain my thinking. You are training their bodies, yes. You are also coaching their minds.

These are the times that measure you as a manager, when the world is falling apart, when all that you have worked for over the course of a long, gruelling season seems lost. These are the moments when you need your players to have faith in you. This is when you stand or fall.

I did not have a long speech prepared for the players. My notes from the game show there was one message, one word, above all others, that I wanted to drill into them. It is written in Spanish.

Lucharlo.

Fight for it.

We would have just a few minutes to prepare the players for the system we intended to play in the second half, with three defenders, two wing-backs, two midfielders – Xabi Alonso and Dietmar Hamann – sitting, protecting us from the runs of Kaka, which had caused us so many problems in the first half, and Steven Gerrard playing just behind Milan Baros.

Hamann would replace Djimi Traore, meaning Jamie Carragher would play on the left of our back three, Sami Hyypia in the middle and Steve Finnan on the right.

'We'll go in, I'll go through the tactics and then you take Hamann out to warm up,' I told my assistant, Pako Ayesterán, as we rushed down the tunnel at the interval.

I was already planning what I was going to say to the players, working out how to express my message in English, to make sure it was as clear and as positive as it needed to be.

'Djimi, have a shower, get changed,' I told him as we reached the stark, white dressing room.

I took a moment to gather my thoughts, before turning to the rest of the team.

'Listen,' I said. What little noise there had been among the players quietened. As a manager, you can tell when your players are looking to you for hope, for inspiration. It was important that I kept calm, presented a confident front. I could not let them think it was over.

The words came easily now, even in a second language.

'We have nothing to lose,' I said. 'If we can relax, we can get a goal. And if we get the first goal, we can come back into the game. We have to fight. We owe something to the supporters. Don't let your heads drop. We are Liverpool. You are playing for Liverpool. Don't forget that. You have to hold your heads high for the supporters. You cannot call yourselves Liverpool players with your heads down. We have worked so hard to be here, beaten so many

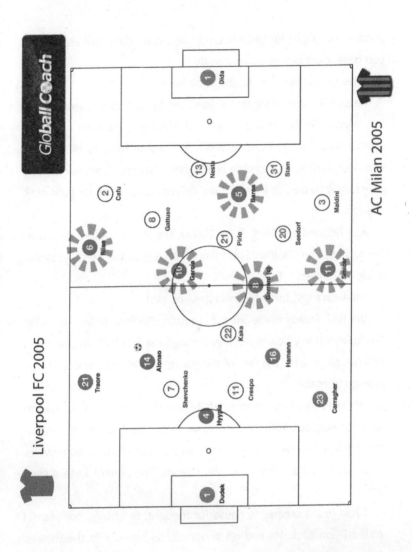

In the second half, we had much more control of the game. We encouraged Riise and Smicer, playing as wing backs, to get forward, so that when Alonso had the ball, he had five options going forward. That enabled us to overload Milan's defence and launch our comeback.

good teams. Fight for forty-five minutes. If we score, we are in it. If you believe we can do it, we can do it.

'Give yourselves the chance to be heroes.'

I explained the changes we would make tactically. Carra on the left, Hyypia in the middle, Finnan on the right. Hamann and Xabi Alonso would sit in front of them. We would have to be narrow, compact, and try to push the line higher. That would allow Milan to play longer passes, so I warned the defenders to watch for balls over the top.

As I finished speaking, Dave Galley, the physio, pulled me aside. He had been working on Steve Finnan on one of the massage tables while I had been talking.

'He won't last forty-five minutes,' he said.

We had already made one substitution, Vladimir Smicer replacing the injured Harry Kewell midway through the first half, and we could not risk playing for the rest of the game, in that heat, with just one change to make.

We only had two minutes left before the players would have to go back out, but without Finnan, we had a problem on the right-hand side. Even now, though, I knew I could not afford to be nervous. You cannot focus when you are nervous. You cannot keep a clear head.

I had just a second to pause for thought, to change our plans. I called Djimi back. He had his boots off, on his way to the shower. Now he would go out for the second half. Finnan would have to come off. You could see in his eyes that he wanted to kill Dave.

Carra would have to switch to the right, with Traore on the left.

Smicer, not a natural winger, would have to play wide on the right in the second half, though eventually Steven Gerrard would replace him there.

'The fans are with us,' I said, as the players started to move towards the door. I do not know if they could hear them singing, 50,000 people bellowing out Liverpool's anthem, 'You'll Never Walk Alone', despite the pain of that first half.

During a game, I am so intensely focused that I cannot even pick out my own family in the crowd. You block everything out. You see only the players, the match. But we all knew how many supporters had made the journey. We had all seen the swathes of Liverpool red in the stands. We knew how long the trip had been, and we knew that we had to fight for them. 'They are behind us.'

The players had endured probably the worst forty-five minutes of their careers. From the first kick, everything had gone wrong. They had one chance to put it right. This was a situation none of us would have dared to imagine. It was not supposed to be like this. All of our hopes rested on the players believing that we had a plan, trusting us to turn things around.

They stood up and started to filter towards the door, towards the tunnel, towards the pitch. Towards history.

Epilogue

BEING A FOOTBALL MANAGER IS NOT JUST A JOB; IT IS AN identity too.

Football has always been my life. As a child, I would, like so many boys my age, play for two or three hours a day with my friends. I loved basketball, too, and I learned judo. My competitive streak meant that I was prepared to give any sport a chance. But football was special, and it remains so.

Why we love the game is not something we often think about, but to me that football is unique is proved by the fact that there are no other games you play with your feet. In rugby, or basketball, or whatever, you use your hands. That makes football different, and more difficult. You have to move yourself and the ball in perfect, fluid motion. It requires not only ability but an understanding of the game, an understanding of the dynamics of the body.

Even as a young player, I would analyse my performance and that of my team. That helped me improve to such an extent that, as a teenager, I was drafted into Real Madrid's youth system. When I went to university, I started coaching; when I was working in a gym, I continued. At twenty-six, I returned to Real and took charge of the club's under-sixteen side.

I approached that job with just as much energy and commitment as I would later give to Tenerife, Extremadura, Valencia, Liverpool and Internazionale. I would often go to the base of the Spanish Football Association at 9.30 in the morning and not leave until well past three in the afternoon. There were three pitches there, and from one spot you could easily take in two games at one time. I would watch the matches taking place for hours, picking up tips, learning about systems, scouting our forthcoming opponents.

All of that information was passed to my teenaged players. We were the best team in Madrid – as was only right for a youth side at Real – but still I would tell them what formation the opposition that afternoon liked to use, what their strengths were, how we could find and exploit their weaknesses. We would use heart monitors to track their conditioning, anything at all we could think of to gain an advantage. That is my competitive streak again. I like to win.

It is something that took me from Real's youth teams to my first jobs as a manager in the senior game, to Valencia, on to Liverpool and, after my time at Anfield came to an end, to Inter.

A few days after my lawyers had agreed a compensation deal with Liverpool, I was approached by representatives of Massimo

Moratti, the Inter owner. During my holiday in Sardinia, I had seen my name linked with the club in the newspapers – along with a number of other contenders – and I was, of course, enormously flattered to be offered the chance to move to San Siro. Inter had just won the Champions League and the Serie A championship, and they had a squad packed full of internationals.

My concern was that the team was growing a little old, that they had passed their peak the previous season, but Moratti and his technical director, Marco Branca, went out of their way to assure me that they were aware of the problem, that I would be given all the support and opportunity I required to start revamping the squad. I outlined my plan: three senior, international-quality players, three young Italian players and three players from abroad, under the age of twenty-one, who would qualify as home-grown in three years' time. That way, the present, the short-term and the long-term future would all be in hand.

The players were equally responsive. I spoke with a number of them before accepting Inter's offer, and they convinced me they still had the hunger to build on all that they had achieved the previous season, under José Mourinho. They insisted there was room to improve their style of play, to win titles and trophies again, but to win them with a more attractive approach. All seemed to be in place: I accepted the job, and moved to Milan.

Our main target that year was the World Club Championship, now moved from Japan to Abu Dhabi. Massimo Moratti's father, Angelo, had won the trophy in 1964 and 1965 – when it was still called the Intercontinental Cup – while in charge of Inter, and the current owner was determined to emulate his achievement.

The club's ability to spend, though, was hampered by their determination to stick to UEFA's Financial Fair Play guidelines – designed to stop teams spending beyond their means and accumulating huge amounts of debt – and they were taken aback when AC Milan, our fierce rivals, signed Zlatan Ibrahimovic on loan from Barcelona, with the transfer to be made permanent later on in the year. It was an enormous coup for Milan, and a considerable blow for Inter: Ibrahimovic, after all, had been one of the club's iconic players just two years previously. Now he would be lining up in the red-and-black of their sworn enemies.

Despite our lack of signings, the season started well on the pitch. We lifted the Supercoppa Italiana, the equivalent of the Community Shield, by beating Roma at San Siro, and by the end of September we were top of the league. By November, only the excellent start made by Lazio was keeping us away from top spot in the table, and we were in a strong position in the Champions League: we had beaten Tottenham 4–3 at San Siro, a game often remembered for a Gareth Bale hat-trick in the second half, but equally notable for Inter's powerful performance before the break.

The most important tournament, though, the whole focus of the season, was in Abu Dhabi. That was the tournament I had been told was to be prioritised above all others. Thankfully, we could deliver Moratti the one prize he coveted above all others.

We defeated the South Korean side Seongnam in the semi-finals, winning 3–0, thanks to goals from Dejan Stankovic, Javier Zanetti and Diego Milito, and defeated the African champions TP Mazembe by the same score-line in the final. Inter, for the first time in forty-five years, were world champions. Moratti had emulated his father, and I had made up for that painful defeat in Japan with Liverpool five years previously.

That was 18 December, and was unquestionably the high point of my Inter career. Everything else at the club was not exactly as it had been advertised in the brochure. Within a week, I was back on Merseyside, after agreeing with the club that it was best that we parted company. My Italian adventure was over before Christmas.

I returned to Liverpool, to West Kirby, to my home. My family were delighted to be back in England, and I decided immediately that I would take some time off. I would not look for another job straightaway, hurling myself back into another challenge. It was time to take a step back, to reflect and recharge.

I am not the sort simply to stay at home, though, watching television. That is fine for a week, maybe two, and perhaps for some people a month, but, as I say, being a football manager is not just a job. It is an identity. It is who I am. Football is my life. I wanted to be involved, and I have found a number of ways to be close to the game.

There is the website, of course, which allows me to analyse certain matches and to offer a few thoughts on the way football is changing, as it always does. I have developed a computer program, an app, to help coaches plan their sessions, arrange their exercises, consider their tactics and set their targets. It was suggested to me that I might like to take to the stage to discuss my time at Liverpool at the city's Empire Theatre, and, of course, there has been plenty of television work, in England and further afield, and the usual stream of media enquiries.

There have been offers of employment, too, clubs tentatively asking whether I am ready to return to work full-time. All of those approaches are immensely flattering, of course, and tempting too: to help a team qualify for the Champions League, or to wrestle a league title away from a fierce rival. None, though, has yet been quite right.

That is not to suggest that I do not still have ambitions, targets, dreams of what I still hope to achieve. Even now, with all of my other commitments, I still manage to watch several games a week, from all over the world. Some I like to analyse tactically, to see how certain teams are doing certain things. Football changes so quickly, with new innovations and systems, and it is important to keep up. But mostly, I watch games looking for players, and instruct my staff to do the same. It is crucial that, as soon as the right offer does arise, I know exactly which players I need for the future, for the challenges that lie in wait.

It is natural, too, to start to think how you would counteract certain teams. I am often asked whether I have a system, or an idea, that I think would be able to beat Barcelona, or Real Madrid, or Manchester City, or Bayern Munich, or Chelsea. Of course, after twenty-five years spent considering how to beat other teams, it is something I have thought about, sketching out ideas in my mind, watching how all of those great sides play and attempting to pinpoint their flaws. You always have thoughts about what you could do against any particular opponent with certain players, in certain circumstances. It is a state of mind that comes naturally to a manager.

My wife, of course, is delighted that I have been at home, helping with the girls, watching them grow up. That has been a pleasure for me, too, to spend more time with my family. A manager's life is an intense one: the hours are long, and there is a huge amount of travel to be undertaken during the season. Often, I would not return home until late in the evening, and my time with my daughters is, of course, precious.

A lot of managers say that they must return to work because their wives want them out of the house; I am sure that is not true of Montse, but she understands that there will come a time when I want to work, and I need to work. Coaching players and managing a team is what I do. It is what makes me happy.

I was professor of physical education at a school, and I think that shows in the way that I work. I have a love for football, but I also love to help improve players, to do whatever I can to make them a little bit better, to pass on what I have learned over the last twenty-five years of coaching.

Some of my former players at various clubs have suggested that I am always on top of them, pushing them, and I suppose that is my style: I am always analysing to see what else they can do, how they can maximise their talent.

That is one of the things that I love most about being a manager, the opportunity to help players improve, and with it improve myself. It is something I would look for in my next job, wherever that may be. It is not simply a matter of identifying which club has the most money, or the best prospects for immediate success: it is most fulfilling to work with a squad, to watch your team grow over time, to build something special.

I want to challenge for titles, to be competitive and to win trophies, of course, as anyone involved in football does. But there is more to it than that. After all, it is not just a job. It is a life.

Index